Creative Writing
Anthology **2010**

Prose,
Life Writing,
Scriptwriting

UEA Creative Writing Anthology 2010
Prose, Life Writing, Scriptwriting

First published by Egg Box Publishing, 2010.

International © retained by individual authors.

This book is sold subject to the condition that it shall not, by way of trade or otherwise, be lent, resold, hired out, stored in a retrieval system, or otherwise circulated without the publisher's prior consent in any form of binding or cover other than that in which it is published and without a similar condition including this condition being imposed on the subsequent purchaser.

A CIP record for this book is available from the British Library.

UEA Creative Writing Anthology 2010 is typeset in Oranda 10.5pt on 13pt Leading.

Printed and bound by:
Printed in Great Britain by the MPG Books Group,
Bodmin and King's Lynn

Designed and typeset by:

Kettle of Fish Design, Norwich
www.kettleoffishdesign.com

Proofed by:
Sarah Gooderson

Distributed by:
Central Books

ISBN:
978-0955939952

Acknowledgements

UEA Creative Writing Anthology 2010

Thanks to the following for making this anthology possible:
the Malcolm Bradbury Memorial Fund, the Centre for Creative and Performing Arts at the University of East Anglia and The School of Literature & Creative Writing at UEA in partnership with Egg Box Publishing.

We'd also like to thank the following people:

Trezza Azzopardi, Jean Boase-Beier, Amit Chaudhuri, Jon Cook, Andrew Cowan, Giles Foden, Sarah Gooderson, Lavinia Greenlaw, Rachel Hore, Kathryn Hughes, Michael Lengsfield, Jean McNeil, Natalie Mitchell, Rob Ritchie, Michèle Roberts, George Szirtes and Val Taylor.

Nathan Hamilton at Egg Box Publishing, and Catrin & Dylan Lloyd-Edwards at Kettle of Fish Design.

Editorial team:
Whitney Austin
Tom Benn
Carrie Chandler
Georgie Codd
Catherine Etoe
Tim Harding
Annabel Howard
Alex Ivey
Julia Webb

UEA Creative Writing Anthology 2010

Contents

Foreword
John Boyne i

Prose
Introduction – Andrew Cowan 8

Contributors
Tom Benn 10
Safia Bhutta 16
Sally Campbell 22
Armando Celayo 28
Georgie Codd 34
Gordon Collins 41
Maire Cooney 46
Edward Dadswell 54
Anna Delany 59
Chelsey Flood 65
Tim Harding 71
Alex Ivey 79
Richard Lambert 85
Ben Lyle 91
Tanya Lyn 97
Retšepile Makamane 103
Andrew Parrott 108
Joshua Piercey 115
Rob Magnuson Smith 120
Sunita Soliar 124
David Strickland 130
Anastasia Tsalta 135
Vicky Warren 140
Eleanor Wasserberg 146
D.W. Wilson 151

Life Writing
Introduction – Kathryn Hughes 158

Contributors
Maddy Tongue 160
Vanessa Morton 166
Cassandra Scott 171
Annabel Howard 176

Scriptwriting
Introduction – Val Taylor 182

Contributors
Whitney Austin 184
Chris Cox 196
Pamela Edwardes 209
James Elliott 222
Jonathan Gillis 229
Sean Gregory 244

UEA Creative Writing Anthology 2010

Foreword

by **John Boyne**

I was only 23 years old when I arrived in Norwich to take up my place as a student on the Creative Writing MA. I didn't know what to expect from the year ahead; to be honest I hadn't given a lot of thought to what I was actually going to write during my time at UEA and came armed with only a couple of half-completed short stories and the rumblings of a novel in my head. Still, I thought, channelling Joe Gargery from *Great Expectations: What larks!*

It was Malcolm Bradbury's last year in charge and we twelve apostles who sat in our black leather *Mastermind* chairs every Wednesday afternoon – there were only a dozen students accepted on to the course then, all aspiring fiction writers, all ambitious, all hoping to become novelists – were in awe of the great man and ready to scribble down even the most minor comments he made about our work. Even the criticisms. (And there were plenty of those.)

It was an exciting time in my life, a year that had as many highs as lows, but looking back now, fifteen years after I graduated, I can see how valuable the course was in shaping the writer that I would become.

At times, however, it felt as if we weren't writers at all, we were statisticians. We knew the average percentage of students who, a decade after completing the course, would be full-time novelists. We looked around the room and calculated how many of us would make it if the statistics of the past were to hold true. The answer? Four. We were very conscious of this figure. *Very.*

But at other times, we were definitely writers. We aimed to impress

with our classroom submissions. We offered each other work outside of our weekly sessions and sat in the bar in the evenings, examining every paragraph, deconstructing every sentence, chipping away at every phrase in order to find ways to make them sound more truthful. We helped each other in extraordinary ways and, it has to be admitted, at times we did the opposite; we were each as capable of unkindness and spite as we were goodwill and support. But we were committed to our work and there was not a person in the room who did not believe in the power of the written word and the sublime beauty of an overwhelming work of fiction.

If I learned one thing from studying at UEA it was this: that it was not enough simply to want to be a writer, I had to know what type of writer I wanted to be. I had to understand my own work. The early writing I did on the course was, at best, derivative of the novelists I admired. Malcolm and my fellow students knocked this out of me fairly quickly, leaving me a little bereft. *So what am I supposed to write now?* I wondered. A question no one could answer but me and even then it took time. But the course equipped me for that and taught me that it took work, focus, commitment and discipline to be a writer. And a little talent too, of course.

This latest anthology of new writing is part of a proud bloodline. Some of the names on the contents page will be read widely over the course of their lifetime. Some will produce extraordinary novels, some will create screenplays that will offer transcendent hours in the dark of a local cinema, others will publish collections of poetry that will come to be seen as works of enriching art. And we get the chance to read them now, before the business of publishing has consumed them, before interviews, book tours and literary festivals have become their way of life. We get to read them when it's all about the words.

JB

John Boyne was a student on the Creative Writing MA at UEA during 1994/95 and Writing Fellow in 2004/05. He is the author of eight novels, including the international bestsellers *The House of Special Purpose* and *The Boy In The Striped Pyjamas*, which sold over five million copies and was made into a Miramax feature film. His latest book is a children's novel, *Noah Barleywater Runs Away*. His books are published in over 40 languages.

UEA Creative Writing Anthology 2010

Prose

Introduction by **Andrew Cowan**

Tom Benn
Safia Bhutta
Sally Campbell
Armando Celayo
Georgie Codd
Gordon Collins
Maire Cooney
Edward Dadswell
Anna Delany
Chelsey Flood
Tim Harding
Alex Ivey
Richard Lambert

Ben Lyle
Tanya Lyn
Retšepile Makamane
Andrew Parrott
Joshua Piercey
Rob Magnuson Smith
Sunita Soliar
David Strickland
Anastasia Tsalta
Vicky Warren
Eleanor Wasserberg
D. W. Wilson

It's a shame we must grade our students' work. The relationship of tutor to student in our 'discipline' (as counter-intuitive a term as can be imagined for so recalcitrant an activity) is often compared to that between editor and author, but no publishing writer would expect her editor to hand down a percentage mark on her work. She would expect, instead, some suggestions for its improvement, applause where it's due, a sense of personal commitment to its development. But while much of our work is indeed editorial in this way, the relationship with our students is also that of writer to writer, which suggests another comparison, that between master and apprentice. But then, for all that a tutor may be more experienced, few of us would claim to have achieved a position of mastery in our craft, and often the issues our students are experiencing – whether of conception or composition – are issues we continue to face. The term that seems best to describe it is mentoring, which implies a sharing of experience rather than any demonstration of mastery. And of course this has always gone on. Long before the 'disciplining' of writing in the academy, writers helped other writers. We still do that. But we also give grades. And if we must, we must, but I prefer to think of these marks as markers, nothing more than pegs on a map. Certain students who score highly now may not need to develop much further. Some who score less well may be the ones who go furthest. It's happened before. And here in this anthology is a record of how far our students have already come – which is far. By the time you read them they will already have lengthened their stride. Before long, some will be overtaking their tutors.

AC

Tom Benn

The Doll Princess
An extract from a crime novel

Manchester, July 1996. One month after the IRA bombing. Bane is a drug pusher and enforcer for a loan shark called Frank. Yesterday, Bane read about the murder of an old school friend turned prostitute and the Manchester killing of a wealthy Egyptian socialite. Both of them were last seen together at Terence Formby's Kitchen Club.

Terence was a crook like Frank, and for rivals, they had a pretty good working relationship – they even had Boxing Day dinner together one year. Wives and all. Terence was about ten years older than Frank but in twice as good shape. He was slim round the waist to say he liked a drink, had a foul mouth, a neat silver head of hair and a good chin. He was newly free of a third trophy wife and it would be a while before he'd settle on a fourth. Terence only ever came out in a flash Hugo Boss suit, polished Italian shoes flooring the pedals of his XK8 or Land Cruiser like he was cock of the walk. Formby earned the most from two nightclub venues. He lived above the first, The Kitchen Club, with its choosy coke-sweating doormen who thumbed-up first division footballers, Page 3 totty and no-names off the box. The second was a grubby strip club, north of the ring road. There may have been more, a massage parlour in Chinatown was rumoured to be his under somebody else's name, but that was all I knew of. He was Salford-born, so it goes. His old man had been a baker.

I nipped back to Frank's to get some decent grub, pinched a special that had been sent back to the kitchen and washed it down with a Kaliber. I didn't see Gordon but on the way out I saw Frank giving one of the foreign chefs a rough time of it – outside behind the cage by the bottle bins. Frank wiped his Brylcreem quiff back into shape. Said a few more nasty words. Polish waiters got fists to the stomach when they cocked up – you don't want to leave a mark on them if they're serving out front. But chefs? They're in the back. No problems at all.

I didn't say hello.

I parked up off St Mary's Parsonage and walked back onto Deansgate. It was just after 11.

The Kitchen Club.

A long queue of tall heels and short frocks. I walked up the line and clocked the meatheads on the door – I was pally with one of the bouncers but it must have been his Saturday off. I lapped round the back and tried my luck on the blue iron door. Some naff house tune throbbed from inside, louder when the peep window slid open: 'Fuck off.'

I said: 'It's one o Frank's boys. I'd like a friendly word with our good Terence.'

'Fuck off.'

'Fair enough, mate. I know where I'm not wanted. Goodbye cruel world.'

'Bane ... '

'Jamie, lad? Didn't see you on the door.'

He opened up. I shook hands with the Silverback in a Crombie.

'That gym needs to start chargin you rent,' I said.

'Lookin all right yerself, these days.'

'Cheers,' I said, still flexing my sore fingers.

'Bin goin this new one outta town, mate. But not bin this week. Not ad much chance with work n that. Fuckin pigs wantin statements from us all about this dead bird – meant two mornins down bloody station. Missin me beauty sleep, mate. It's bin all go down ere though, a tell yer.'

'I bet.'

Jamie's eyeballs worked faster than his tongue. He looked like he could do with laying off the charlie tonight. I followed his fridge-freezer

of a back. He could have given our Gordon a good run for his money.

This way in took you behind the bar and led upstairs to a staffroom and up again to Formby's posh flat. The warped subwoofers from the club made it sound like we were inside an over-crowded womb. These were plush for back-of-club rooms.

Jamie took me over to a curvy bird in a plain green frock at the bottom of some carpeted stairs. She was about thirty-five with a hard face, a 300-watt tan bed complexion and a clipboard. She had a fancy haircut that was upset by a daft microphone headpiece that looked more for show than anything.

'Is that thing switched on?' I said to her.

'Is it bugger,' Jamie said. 'But don't she look fab? Shell, tek im up to see Terence if ee's decent ... is ee decent?'

'I want plannin on checkin,' she went. She looked me over with a practised coldness and said: 'He's up there havin a bit of a private get-together. It's your funeral, chick.'

'You'd look good in black,' I said.

Her mouth twisted into a smile.

*

I waltzed in solo. Formby had a swanky big pad and I followed the boom of his voice to an open living room. The music in the club downstairs couldn't be heard from up here. Not even a vibration.

'Bane, int it?'

'Spot on.'

'Shell jus told us you were poppin up.'

'Yeah, that's right.'

He shook my hand and dropped it. 'Sit down, son. Get yourself a fuckin drink. I hear you came in through the back?'

There was charlie and booze and a pack of cards spread on the glass coffee table. Plenty of cash. I sat down on a sofa seat and picked up a bottle of brandy by the neck and read the label. 'Didn't fancy the queues.'

'Don't fuckin blame you. Should've rang us before. Someone would've got you on the guest-list.'

'I'm here now.' I put the brandy back down.

'How's our Frank doin?' Terence said.
'Well. He's very well.'
'Good to hear, son. Bet he don't know how to party like this though, does he? That fat bugger can't even get in his bloody catsuit no more. Shake, rattle and sausage roll.'
We all made sure we laughed.
The we: a coked-up local TV weatherman, two councilmen and a first division midfielder plus his tagalongs. There were some other fruity lounge lizards and local crooks mooching here and there – small-time, still saving up for the Cheshire home and second-hand Beamer.
There were also a good five or six clearly trafficked Eastern European girls willowing about the room in shaky stilettos, a couple with their bony arses on some tub of lard's pinstriped knee, each one doped to the nines. Gloomy things. They looked like broken dolls.
And then there was this one sat to my right.
This one was glamorously thin. All lips and eyes and cliff-edge cheekbones, a drainpipe torso lost somewhere inside a flimsy taupe mini-dress. Hair was dark blonde, cut just above shoulder length and moussed back savagely into place. Her earrings were Cyndi Lauper dangly shells and crosses – a Eurotrash giveaway.
I stretched an arm out on the sofa back and brushed her shoulder. Her face made its way round to mine in no hurry, huge slate eyes working a steady blinking pattern. I didn't fancy my chances in a staring contest.
'That a scar, a tat or a birthmark?' My hand moved down to the top of her arm. I traced around the plum crown shape on her skin with an index finger.
'Don't bother, lad,' Terence went, refilling his drink. 'She don't know a fuckin word o Queen's English. Not a fuckin word.'
'Did Baz bring her round?' I said.
Terence sat back with a full glass. 'Who?' He tightened his face.
'That slimy sod mithers Frank every other week.'
He gave me the benefit of the doubt. 'There were a time when that Baz might bring a girl or two down to the club. Filthy slags, dear me. But how could he compete with this?' He held his arms out like he was offering me it all.
'And where does all this new crumpet live?'

'Why? You thinkin about takin one home to meet your mam?'

I slapped my heart. 'My poor mam's gone, Terence.'

'Shame, cos I'd recommend it. They won't show you up, don't even answer back.'

The midfielder roared with phoney laughter.

Terence leaned forward again. 'You couldn't afford these, son. So enjoy um now while you can. Cos I'd be careful.'

'How d'you mean?'

'You not read the news? Dead Safir n that missin wog that lived on her shoulder? Made the nationals this mornin.'

'Saw a bit in the locals yesterday.'

'That fairy Abdul doin a runner. Fuckin daft paki.'

'Knew her well did you? Safir.'

'She liked it down here. We gave her a table.'

'And who's got it now?'

He didn't say anything to that.

I spotted a closed circuit camera in the top far corner of the room. 'Beefin up security nowadays?'

Formby tried to smile: 'Pigs've bin at the CCTV to see who she left with. But our new security system hasn't bin workin proper. We jus got it up n runnin yesterday. Smile, lad. Candid camera.' He turned and pointed up at the cam. I looked straight at it. 'Give us a wave, Bane,' he said.

A bit much. The flat, as well as the club. I turned away. 'I never met Safir, myself. What was she like then, ay? Worth a go?'

'I tek it you don't know then?'

'I tek it I don't,' I said – like I was hanging off his every fucking word.

Formby's face screwed up as he gave his next words a dress rehearsal in his head first. 'Obnoxious little cow. Jus soddin perfect. You'd wanna cut her jus to knock the smile off her face. You know that type? Yeah – y'do don't you? Course he does. She was young n loaded n a right looker n fuckin rotten on the inside. Open that one up n we're talkin maggot factory, son.'

'Somebody did.'

'Ay?'

'Open that one up.'

'Fuckin aye.'

'What was her poison?'

He took a big swig and knocked the lot back. Refilled. 'Shaggin, Bane. She loved shaggin. Not jus coke. Not whizz. Not jus spendin her daddy's cash. Shaggin. Safir the fuckin sex monster. Jus wait till them tabloids get wind.'

At the rate Terence was blabbing, that wouldn't be too far off. God bless the charlie.

So I tried my luck: 'She was bein blackmailed then?'

He pulled a passing bird down into his lap. 'Steady. You've only been here ten minutes n you're already life o the party. What's with all this diggin, lad?'

'I'm not diggin.'

'You are!' he said, slapping the girl's grey thigh for emphasis, drink swinging in his other hand. 'I'm nursin a bloody semi here n you're makin me chat bout this bollocks. What the fuck are we doin?' He raised his glass. 'Let's fuckin av it!'

The lads cheered. The dolls didn't get a vote.

I looked into the face of the skinny bird with the birthmark next to me. There wasn't a glimmer of involvement. Not a thing.

Terence settled down and said to me with a shark grin: 'Now stay, have a drink, have a laugh or fuck off.'

About an hour later and Terence was already a goner. He was rolling around on his Egyptian carpets, crying with laughter, knocking over his own vases and imported brandy bottles. Most of the broken dolls had lost their clothes.

Tom Benn graduated from UEA in 2009 with a first in English Literature with Creative Writing and won the Malcolm Bradbury Bursary to do the Creative Writing MA. He grew up in South Manchester.

Safia Bhutta

The Event of Rapture

One: Ghana

After Greg's funeral Patrick sat on the warm sand, his back against the wooden ribs of the bar. He watched the waves slap the shore and decided he wasn't going to be buried like that.

A breeze clinked through the crate of empty bottles on the counter above him. This stupid place – more than a year of twelve-hour days and what had they managed? Around him beach huts loomed, doorless and roofless in the semi-dark, ringed by knee-high coconut palms: *the Sweet Arcadia Lodge.*

Jenny and Florence had retreated into the house, the only finished building on site. They took a clutch of women with them, ex-pats and Ghanaians – and Greg's mother of course. Sixty-four years old. She'd never been in the country before, never got past the Sahara. Greg and Florence used to meet her once a year up in Morocco. She barely looked older than her daughter-in-law.

The remaining mourners clustered round a picnic table out by the sea, the glow of their cigarettes becoming brighter as the light faded.

The beer had run out. Patrick should have known to buy more beer, and more food – only clean skewers and dirty plates left.

A figure detached himself from the picnic table and began to walk up the beach. He should have done more for Florence, Patrick thought, but

what could he do? When he saw Florence on the edge of tears he felt like a child. He wanted to run.

The man was getting closer, drawing up in slow, laboured steps.

'There's nothing left,' Patrick shouted, he waved his empty hands. 'It's all finished – I'm sorry.' Some old English bastard. Did Greg really like them? These old white men: relics with thin smiles and thinner attempts at liberalism, who drove imported Toyotas and stayed inside on Independence Day.

'You are Patrick?' The man called, still a few metres from the bar.

'There's nothing left, I'm sorry. I didn't buy enough.'

'Patrick, yes, Patrick. They say you are here.' He drew up, looking down at Patrick with black eyes set in creased and shadowed skin. He began to lower himself down.

'I shall sit with you.'

Not English after all. Patrick couldn't place the accent, French? German? Something Eastern European maybe? His receding hair was pulled back into a tight ponytail.

'So you don't know me, Patrick?' The man lent in close. So close Patrick could feel the frantic beat of his heart.

'No, at least I don't think so.' Was he supposed to remember every friend Greg had mentioned? Every ex-pat from Takoradi to Accra? He knew he should have gone back to the house with Jenny and the others.

'You will know me when I say my name: Maurice.'

Maurice. Of course, Maurice. The French pronunciation familiar, remembered – *More-reece*.

'You know it yes?'

Of course he had heard of Maurice. The name lit a wild flare of associations: the house Greg described, half ruined in the hills above Accra, the veranda, the wrought iron table, the aniseed reek of Pastis. Girls laughing out of sight, the shriek of monkeys in the cashew trees.

'You will know it.' Maurice sucked a *tsk* sound between his teeth and set an unlabelled bottle down in the strait of sand between their outstretched legs.

'Gin,' he said, 'from London – especially for you.'

'Thanks.'

'You must have some first.'

Safia Bhutta

'I'm all right thanks.'

Maurice picked up the bottle. Patrick half-closed his eyes. He heard the seal rip and the cap twist up the threaded glass.

'Please have some, to help me.'

Patrick took a swallow; neat gin coated his mouth like oily syrup. He would be helpless now, he knew – prisoner to another man's memories, another man's version of Greg.

'These days I see, Greg does not mention me.'

'He might have once or twice.'

'Maybe it is that he is not allowed to mention me.' Maurice took a handful of sand and let it run out between his fingers. 'I knew him when he first came, his first time in Africa. When he was young – he was such a beautiful young man, so much alive – we would be together all day. We work: on the car, on my house – my house is very old. Every time we finish something, he does not stop, he does not sleep. No he is there, this little English voice: "*What now, Maurice? What else can I do? What's next?*"'

'He built this with me.' Patrick gestured into the darkness.

'Yes I know, I know – and he will not stop, will he, Patrick?'

'Only when Florence made him come in for meals.'

'He still came to see me every year.'

'You live in Accra?'

'In Aburi – Greg, he stayed with me – six months when he first came. And Florence as well.'

'I don't know it, Aburi,' Patrick said, though instantly he could picture the verdant hills: the lapsed town where the tarmac road turned to washboard track.

'But then, *of course*, they must move down to Accra. They work they live. Greg comes out of the city at the weekend – every few weeks at least.' Maurice took a swig from the bottle. '*Of course* it is not enough. *Of course* they must move away further, to the East. Then I see Greg once a year, just one or two days. Florence, she has everything she wants.' The loose skin around Maurice's neck shifted as he spoke, pulling against the grip of his shirt collar.

'Florence invited you.'

'Only now, now he is dead, she lets me come.'

Laughter burst from the picnic table and was shushed out. Patrick had never heard Florence mention Maurice. Maurice belonged to Greg's past, to the dazzle of youth and adventure.

'Of course you must know how much he loved to drive,' Maurice said quietly.

Patrick nodded: 'I just – I always thought of him as a lucky man.'

'Ha! Yes but everybody is lucky, Patrick, until the day they are not.'

'I suppose.'

'It is worse for Florence.'

'I know.' Patrick could not blur the vision of the coffin, lowered headfirst so that for a moment it stood almost vertical in the grave, before the other end thumped down onto compact sand.

Maurice shook his head. 'These guys, they drive: no lights, *pas de freins*, mobile in one ear. Silly boys. There is a risk for anyone – always.'

'I keep wondering if he saw it coming. If he knew.' Patrick began to cry. He kept the tears as silent as he could. He couldn't help it. It should have been Greg, not Maurice, settled beside him in the sand.

Someone in the house opened a window and a bass voice pitched out across the beach.

'When this world began, it was heaven's plan
There should be a girl for every single man –'

'She is lucky there are no children,' Maurice said.

'Lucky?'

'They will not remind her of him.' Maurice picked up the bottle, his eyes ahead, and drank, lips not touching the glass. 'You are married, Patrick?'

'Yes –'

'– You have children?'

'I – well not yet.' In six weeks he and Jenny would be on a flight to Heathrow. Home. They'd made half-hearted plans to have the child in Ghana, but Jenny's mother sent plane tickets: open returns. 'She still thinks hospitals in Africa are refugee camps,' Jenny had said. They joked about it, but still, they were going. 'And you, do you have ...'

'Of course, I have many. I am an old man.' Maurice seemed to re-grasp his point. 'But when you, Patrick, when you have a son, you must call him Greg.'

Patrick had considered it – even before, he had fantasised about it: they wouldn't tell Greg until afterwards, a phone call from hospital, Greg's speechless, unbounded, delight. But Jenny had never liked the plan and Patrick repeated her words to Maurice:

'Wouldn't that be a bit hard on Florence?'

'You will have to try more than that I think, to make life harder for Florence.'

'I suppose.'

'Ama, my wife, she says a woman in a crowd is lonelier than a man on his own.'

'What does that mean?'

Maurice shrugged. 'It's just what she says.'

The men around the picnic table began to move off. Three or four came within metres of the bar, but once they'd glanced over they didn't stop, drawn towards the lights of the house. He was going to be left with Maurice, Patrick thought, the bottle was still two-thirds full.

'We should be getting in,' he said.

'Florence, she made a mistake with the funeral.'

'It's really getting dark now.'

'Too quiet. You know what they like round here – billboards and dancing, songs and T-shirts,' Maurice waved his arms as he spoke. '*La grande soirée.*'

Patrick did not reply, Maurice must be at least sixty, he thought. Was there any reason in that? That this man should have already lived for fifteen years longer than Greg.

'She will not stay.'

'Sorry?'

'Florence, she will not stay. I heard she is going to visit someone – a holiday in England.'

'Her sister. They said that at the service; it's not a secret.'

'And you are so very sure she will come back?'

'I think – I think I can't imagine what she's going though.'

'Why not?'

'I'm sorry?'

'No, it's very proper. You are a very proper English man indeed.'

'I'm sure Florence will come back, she loves it here – she lives here.'

'And Greg, of course, is here.' Maurice spoke softly.

'Yes.'

'No. She will not come back.'

Patrick was tired of this. 'How would you know? You know her so well – what, just because she didn't like you when she was twenty-one? I've lived a mile from her for the last year, I see her everyday, I talk to her.'

'Oh yes, you live here. Here, altogether happy in your little *Arcadia*, your little dream. You think that is real, a year of dreaming?'

'It's a dream you're sitting in.'

Maurice laughed. He shifted round to face Patrick. In the dark his pupils and irises had blurred together, black on white.

'Florence. Pah Florence,' he rolled the 'r'. 'She will stay or she will go. She stays – bang – like that she is old. An auntie for baby Greg. A mummy for all the boys and girls who come and stay at this great resort. She will buy them sun cream and tell them to pull up their socks.' Maurice curled his lip at this version of Florence. 'Then, one night – maybe a year, maybe less, Jenny is away, and that night Florence will stay up and get drunk – a little drunk like we are now. Then she will come to your house and she will fuck you. She will fuck you, then she will fuck through everyone you know: your friends, your chef, your waiters –'

'You're disgusting.' But Patrick did not have the courage to exclaim, only to breathe out the words.

'You think that you know this woman. A year? I know her for fifteen years. This type of English woman, I know her.'

Patrick stood up, as he did he felt a rush of cool air from the sea.

'Yes, yes, you go. But you make sure she goes to England, Patrick. You make sure she goes straight away. She does not care about this place – you will have the house, the business, everything. She can cry out her eyes on her sister's shoulder; she can live there – the rest of her life. Send her back to the fucking freezing island where she belongs.'

Safia Bhutta is a trained archaeologist who has travelled and worked in Britain, Europe, West Africa and the Middle East. She is currently working on her first novel, set in England and Ghana.

Sally Campbell

Burnt Island

The following is an edited extract from Burnt Island, a novel. The narrator, Isobel, is an auxiliary nurse working in a psychiatric ward.

I first saw Angie sitting in a green plastic garden chair up against the fence, catching the last of the sunlight as it retreated beyond Ward Twelve's perimeter. She was leaning forward, shaking her head. Her thick plastic-rimmed glasses dangled on a gold chain from her neck. From where I stood inside, I could see the sheen of her pink lipstick but I couldn't make out the words she spoke. She was on her own.
   You have to watch that one.
   The voice startled me, it was so close. I turned to find Victor's face just a little too close to mine, poised, peering out at her.
   Makes allegations, Victor said, looking at Angie. You just have to look at her the wrong way and it's sexual assault.
   I could see the gleaming domes of spots pushing their way up through his reddened skin.
   Well, he said, clasping my shoulders and turning me ninety degrees away from the window, now you've seen the courtyard, let's carry on the guided tour this way.
   I felt myself being pushed down the long carpetless corridor.

*

Victor's shift was over and he had gone home. I walked through

empty rooms. Nothing moved. The ward was a jumble of things left half-done. Objects strewn around: a tented book, spine bent, face down on the arm of a chair, three empty cups huddled on a table surface in front of three empty seats. People had been and gone. And argued: the sugar bowl was upside down in a corner, in a little white dust heap, a trail scattered behind. A toppled chess game sprawled over the dining room floor. I removed a sticky bishop from a cup of orange squash.

Before long, I was back where I had started. The courtyard door opposite stood open and Angie was looking up at me smiling.

You look like someone who's strayed from the path, darling, she said.

I don't know what I'm meant to be doing.

She just smiled. I wasn't sure if she had heard me.

You seen Burdock? she said.

I think he's in the smoking room.

Probably in the smoking room.

Mind if I join you?

Come join me if you like.

The gravel scrunched under my weight. I took another patio chair from the stack behind her and spoke louder this time. It's a beautiful day isn't it?

She didn't respond. The chair sank into the gravel as I sat.

Beautiful day, don't you think? Angie said.

How British, I said quietly to myself.

That's true, she said.

I looked at her. It took a minute to register. Volume wasn't an issue.

I'm Isobel, I said slowly, watching her as I spoke. She leant in and down, reading my lips.

Good to meet you, I'm Angie. She grinned so widely as she said her own name that she closed her eyes. She extended her skinny hand and five long red nails. The skin of her palm was soft and warm.

So how did you end up in here, my darling?

I could ask you the same thing, I said, stringing out the sentence and overly shaping each word for her intent eyes.

Her laughter was more of a high-pitched cackle. Well, my girl, that's a story. Oh yes. A story indeed. She grinned. Footsteps crunched on gravel.

What's the old peacock shrieking about?

Sally Campbell

Angie looked up, still smiling.

Isobel darling, meet Dorian. Dorian, this is Isobel.

Dorian delicately smoothed back his blond hair and straightened his tweed coat. Another handshake. Brisk, strong.

Isn't she sweet? Angie brushed a hand over my head. She's Scottish.

I shot her a look.

Welcome to hell, he said. I trust you disposed of your hopes in the bin provided at the entrance.

I looked up expecting a smile. His eyes pinned me to my seat for a second. I looked away.

Well, if you grow weary of this stuttering, tongue-tied race, and need someone to talk with, not at, my room is number eleven.

Up all hours too, Angie said with a nod of her head. He calls it having twilight afflictions.

Dorian just looked at me.

You've got to watch this one, my love, Angie said. He's a charmer.

And this one, Dorian said jutting his chin out at Angie, can lip read accents.

Two tweed shoulders shrugged, then two pink satin ones replied. Dorian strode away on his spindly legs. Angie put a hand on my arm, not smiling for the first time.

You can't trust anyone in this place.

*

A few hours later I found myself in the smoking room. The balding carpet was scarred with burn marks. Armchairs seemed to lean against each other for support, in different shades of brown and different stages of collapse. Light fell from the high windows in three slanting pillars, but the corners were in shadow. The air was thick enough to smoke. Noises of people passing on down the hall sounded muffled and far away. An upright sat against one wall and I wondered what it would sound like if I opened the lid and struck a note. The room was empty until he spoke.

My father was a beekeeper.

Dorian lent forward, his elbows resting on his thighs. He looked thinner without his jacket. His shirt was unbuttoned and untucked, his

sleeves rolled back showing bony wrists. With one hand, he plucked at his lip while in the other, a cigarette smoked itself to ash. He breathed deeply, staring at the carpet between his feet.

A quiet man, he said and cleared his throat. On summer nights, he would be gone, tending to the bees. There were eighteen, maybe twenty hives, which stood side by side in the heather, up on the hill behind our house. There was something forlorn about them, like desanctified gravestones – overgrown, solemn and dull. They didn't look like much.

I didn't know what to say.

I remember when they arrived, he said and sniffed. They were stir crazy after hours in the back of the van. My uncle was lifting down one of the hives and dropped it. The wooden back fell off and they swarmed all over him. My father told him not to run. They were all over him. He just stood there, swearing as they stung him. When it finally became unbearable, he ran. You almost couldn't recognise him with the swelling. And he was left with little flecks of scarring around his eyes and down his neck. The worst of it was on his back but I never saw it. My father was all right though – he wore the hat and netted mask. But I don't think the stings bothered him anyway because he always had a few on his hands. He just went about his business. It really didn't interest me.

He tapped the ash onto the carpet, put his cigarette to his lips and took a sharp drag, half closing his eyes. He did this twice more, just as quickly, until there was only filter left, which he stubbed out on the arm of the chair. We both reached for the cigarette packet. He looked up but didn't seem to see me. He shook out a cigarette and put it to his lips with shaky fingers. He snatched it out again and fumbled it in his hand.

What are the hives like?

Each hive was roughly two feet long by about nine inches, he said and gestured the shape in the air with his hands. Inside there were about eight flat wooden frames, which separate out the comb. In the wild, I suppose they would all connect, but this way you can pull one section out at a time. The frames slotted in and hung down. The bees built on them, filling them up little by little, sealing each hollow with wax. On they go, until the whole thing is full. And on you go, emptying it of honey.

As he talked, he didn't look up. I watched his eyes sweep the room,

Sally Campbell

coming to rest on one of his shoes.

You're depriving the bees of their food source, so you have to feed them. There were these ceramic jugs. Big heavy jugs that he filled with sugar and water then left, one in each hive. One winter, the weather was cruel, the rain seemed endless, and, for the first time, he forgot about his bees. My mother had just died. So the jugs lay in disuse and the bees had nothing to eat. He nearly lost them all that year. They would've got wet as well you see, and a disease probably spread through the hives. But some survived and new queens hatched. That's when they swarm, you can only have one queen per hive, and she'll take maybe half the hive with her. They never go far though in the first movement. In the wild, they will go a couple of hundred feet and then stop, maybe overnight, in a tree or in the eaves of a house. They will travel for miles the second time round, until they find the right place to settle. In our case, they just moved along the row to the next prefab home, so it was easy to build the hives back up again.

How long do bees live, usually?

The drones last about six to eight weeks. But the queen, she lives years. She has a chamber of her own where she lays and lays. That is all she does, hour after hour. She can live two, maybe three years. Until a young queen eats her.

He ruffled a hand through his hair.

So, if you didn't want them, what happened to the hives?

He looked up, but not at me, narrowing his eyes. He shifted in his seat and fixed on a point just above my head.

One night, I went up onto the hill, into the heather. Petrol sloshed inside the old rusty can I had taken from the garage. I used to love the smell of petrol. I walked up and down the row, swinging my arm because the can really was heavy, dousing each hive. You could hear the hum they made, like a song. I emptied the entire can. I lit a match, threw it, stood well back. I had to throw a good few more. One by one the hives caught. Then I ran. I didn't turn but I could hear the bees and the flames. I fell into the heather to watch. You could see the blaze and the smoke from a long way off. It didn't last as long as I wanted it to.

He frowned and looked down at the unlit cigarette in his hand. He slid it back into the pack. He picked up the three flat stubs he had tossed onto

the carpet, which lay round his feet. He stood and threw one at a time, in a high arc, out of one of the windows. Then he walked out of the room. I listened to the hum of the hive.

*

Eyes flickered, limbs twitched, jigsaw pieces were put down: the trolley had arrived. It trundled down the hallway. I mapped its journey by the sound of the wheels squeaking – cutlery clattered as it turned the corner into the dining room. The still, quiet ward was now a mass of ticks.

There was no line, the queue was more like a jumble of people angled in the same direction. The hatch swung open. Bottles were unstoppered, jars shaken, liquids measured, pills counted. Each colourful offering snatched and then swallowed. I fetched a water jug and some plastic cups for the table in the hall, let them help themselves.

You sleeping yet? I asked Dorian as he strode towards the table.

With dreams like these, and he opened out his hand to show two round blue pills and one triangular green one, who needs sleep?

He tossed them into his mouth, filled a cup and took a drink. His shoulders relaxed, he smiled, placed the cup gently on the table and looked me in the eye.

Table for two, please.

Sally Campbell was born in Stirling, Scotland. She is currently writing her first novel, *Burnt Island*, and a collection of short stories, *Show Me Where To Look*. While at UEA, she was awarded the Malcolm Bradbury Bursary.

Armando Celayo

Satan Beating His Wife

Here's the deal: the first and only time I kicked it with Mike my brother – sorry, half-brother – I was supposed to clock in four hours of English lit classes at summer school. While my friends were sharpening their Playstation skills, I biked from the poor part of north Oklahoma City to the even poorer southside. So I wouldn't stress her out, I told my mom I was headed to class. It was between her morning and evening work shifts and she was having her afternoon siesta. "Sta bueno,' she said. 'Vete con cuidado.'

I'd always known my father had two families (for me, it was an ugly fact of life), but since he'd left my mom – his mistress – about five years ago, Mike was my only connection to him.

By the time I made it to McDonald's, I was half an hour late. Coming in from the heat, my sweat dried out into a second skin. I looked around and found Mike sitting near the back, wiping a little boy's mouth with a napkin. It was only the second time I'd seen him.

Eight days before, I'd gone to El Chino on Twenty-third Street for a checkup. El Chino wasn't Chinese but a Vietnamese doctor named Quảng Nguyen. He was only good for checkups and sleep-depriving antibiotics, but he spoke passable Spanish, so every Latino not wanting a curandera came to him. Those were our only choices back then: hack doctors and phony folk healers.

After I filled out a patient form, I sat in the semi-full waiting room, flipping through a two-year-old copy of *Newsweek*. The place didn't smell clean or dirty, but somewhere in-between – sterile. After forty minutes,

El Chino opened the door to the examination office and said, 'Tijerina. Ramiro Tijerina.' Both Mike and I stood up. We looked at each other. He mad-dogged me as he walked away with El Chino. I took a seat, heated that I'd gotten punked on, yet too pussy to do anything but fill out another form.

When Mike came out, he introduced himself and asked if I was named after my father.

'Yeah,' I said.

'Me, too.'

Mine is one of those old world, multisyllabic names you'd hear on a Mexican telenovela. Up to that point, I'd never met anyone with it. After a long second, I figured out what Mike was getting at: we shared the same father.

In the vinyl booth at McDonald's, Mike saw me and head-upped me over.

'You want anything?' he asked as I sat across from him.

Before I left the house, I'd finished off a cheese-and-Cheetos sandwich and a bottle of orange Gatorade (some folks have childhood relics like teddy bears for comfort – I have orange-colored food). A heatwave held the city in check; I hoped it'd take a five-minute smoke break. When I got to Cowtown, a district thick with the shit-stench of livestock, the food I ate started sloshing around my stomach. What the heat and smell started, anxiety finished. All fucked with me until I threw everything up in a translucent red juice with mushy yellow chunks. 'I'm good,' I said to Mike. 'I had something before I came.'

He stabbed a fry into a blob of ketchup on a burger wrapper. I searched for resemblances between us: other than the same brown eyes, our ears were kind of similar: they stuck out like opened car doors. On his right forearm, he had a Jesus piece tattooed; on his left, ■■■■■■■ and POR VIDA in Olde E letters. 'Was that a girl's name?' I asked.

'Yeah.' Looking at my backpack, he asked what high school I went to.

'Northwest,' I said.

He pointed at himself and said, 'Capitol Hill. You in the smart classes or the dumb ones?'

In the English lit course I was taking, the books worked on me like Tylenol PM every time I opened them. In theory, I was an honors student,

Armando Celayo

but in reality I got my ass handed to me by the simplest of metaphors. 'I'm the dumb kid in the smart classes,' I said.

I caught Mike's little boy staring at me.

'Daddy, who's that?' he asked.

Mike looked at me. 'No one,' he said. 'Just one of daddy's friends.'

Pretending I was comfortable at home and not facing my recently-met half-brother, I smiled at Mike's son.

'What's your name, little man?' I asked. The boy ignored my question and continued inspecting me.

'Michael,' Mike replied. 'But I call him Junior. It's my middle name – after my grandpa.'

'Why don't you go by Ramiro? You're named after him, aren't you?'

'You couldn't pay me enough to use my dad's name. What about you – Ramiro? Junior?'

No one ever called me Junior. The people who mattered most to me (my mom, my aunt and uncles) endeared me as Mijo – son. Sure, my friends and teachers called me Ramiro, but it didn't bug me as much, I could tell, as it did Mike. Sitting in front of him, I didn't want to be named after someone who'd fucked around a lot of people – especially my mom. I summoned a name from the books I was reading for class. 'No – Ishmael,' I said. 'Ish.'

'Finish your food,' Mike said to his son. Junior picked two soggy pickles out of his cheeseburger and scraped the onion-spotted ketchup against the edge of the table. He smelled what was left of his burger; apparently satisfied, he plugged it into his mouth.

'What kind of music you bump?' Mike asked.

'Outkast, lately.'

'Dog, I heard they were dick smokers.'

We both laughed.

'You're crazy,' I said. 'They're just Southern. What do you listen to?'

'Bone.'

'Bone? You say that like it's something to be proud of.'

We laughed a little more.

'Man, they haven't been good,' I said, 'since they were cracked-out Satan worshippers.'

Laughing, Mike shook his head and said, 'Aw, fuck you, bastard.'

That last one lingered in the air.

'My bad,' he said. 'I didn't mean to –'

'I'm going to get some pop. You want a refill?'

He looked at the table and pushed his cup towards me. 'Thanks,' he said.

If things were different, Mike and I might've grown up together. We'd spend summer afternoons grilling carne asada and washing that down with salt-sprinkled watermelon. He'd let me hang out with him and his friends, mostly to do embarrassing shit to make them laugh. With Mike, books wouldn't matter. We'd run the streets, kicking lampposts until they shuttered off, leaving us in darkness. He'd start dating then come home late at night, asking me to sniff his fingers. Guess where that smell came from? He'd mess around until, unplanned, one of his girls got pregnant – one he never actually really even liked but nonetheless whispered into her ears R&B song lyrics twisted into his version of seduction. It'd work out between them for four or five – hell, maybe even six – years. He'd get restless, by then probably having another kid. A son, of course – two boys. The things he'd do so he wouldn't have to be at home with his wife: pick up extra shifts at work, drink Coors Light over at his friends' house, take me out to the dollar movies. Finally, on the downlow, he'd start fucking some high school girl working the checkout at El Mariachi Taquería. The mistakes of this world escape into that one.

I bought my drink and refilled Mike's. At the soda machine, I looked over and saw him holding up his palms so Junior could slapbox them. Thinking of my father and the bastard-bomb Mike had just dropped, I covered one of my nostrils and blew an orange wad of snot into his cup.

'How is he?' Mike asked when I returned. 'My dad.'

'I don't know. I haven't seen him in a while.'

'Oh. I thought when he left us, he moved in with you.'

Mike told me that our father, a Mexican immigrant, only married his mother so he could stay in the country. Her folks were fourth-generation Oklahomans from Ireland, and against the whole thing. For as long as he could remember, Mike's parents weren't happy with each other; every morning he found them sleeping in different rooms.

While Mike recounted this, I stared at Junior. He dumped the contents of his Happy Meal onto the table. Some fries fell out, along with a sugar

cookie in the shape of a headless Ronald McDonald, and a plastic bag containing a racecar.

'Did you know he was a roofer?' Mike asked.

'No. I just remember he drove a big truck.'

'Most people run away from hurricanes – he ran to them chasing work. One year, Florida got hit so he packed some clothes and drove down. He wired money every other week. After a while, he stopped.'

'How long ago was this?'

'I don't know. Maybe ten years ago.'

I recalled the stubbled cheek I'd kissed goodbye as a child, after my father spent the entire afternoon with us and was about to go back to his rightful family. By the way she held his hand, I could tell my mom didn't want to let him go. I felt like I should tell Mike my side of things, but my father's other family – me and my mom – were nothing but invalids.

Mike's beeper went off. Reading the screen, he said to his son, 'Quit playing. Your mommy needs us to pick her up from work.' Junior was sucking on a mouthful of fries.

We walked out and loitered by the door. It was raining, though there weren't any gray puffs above us. I held out my hand and heavy drops pelted my palms. The water was cool as it fell, but it evaporated once it hit the hot pavement. The air was humid, like the thickness that seeps out of a just-finished dishwashing load. I knew I'd have to bike through it.

'I always thought they were crazy,' Mike said.

'What?'

'Sunshowers.'

I remembered something my mom said, a phrase she picked up after twenty-some-odd years in Oklahoma. 'Satan beating his wife,' I said.

'Huh?'

'Satan beating his wife. It's what they say when it's a perfectly good day outside, but it's raining all the same.'

Mike looked at the sky then said, 'That shit makes no sense. Why would Satan have a wife?'

At a grocery story across the street, people were sprinting, pushing their shopping carts in front of them, while the others – the lucky ones,

I guess, who had someone to look out for them – waited under the shelter near the entrance. I said, 'I don't know, man. I don't know.'

Armando Celayo's work has appeared in *PEN International*, *World Literature Today*, and elsewhere. He is the fiction editor of *Molossus*, an online broadside. He has also worked with the Flaming Lips and Stardeath and White Dwarfs. He is completing a book titled *Fading Portraits of Martyred Saints*.

Georgie Codd

Cakery

Martin, Michelle and Diane

Cakery

The cake sits on a porcelain platter: a light, porous sponge, yellowed by dark yolks; three layers, equally-spaced, separated by thick clumps of buttercream icing. A flourish of juicy-ripe berries pokes shyly from the edges. On the top lies a cloud of sifted icing sugar, which has spilled generously onto the table.

She has never loved a cake before. There have been plenty of predecessors – dozens baked by her own cool hands – but nothing like this. Years have gone into this cake.

It's a he-cake. She can tell, easily. The dark, vanilla-like flecks which pepper its sponges. The sharp, royal tang of blueberry. Crimson bleeding, indecently, from crushed raspberries. In her mouth it will feel solid and dense, and the cream will cloy at the back of her throat.

She wants him now, before the rest of them arrive. He belongs to her. Not a cake to be shared: there has been enough sharing.

She wets a finger with the tip of her tongue and dabs it, gently, into a dense mound of sugar. Imagining his enjoyment, she licks the residue off her skin and repeats the gesture in a different place. When finished she observes her work. She has given him eyes. Two blank spaces, peering from a dusty canvas: the beginnings of a face. She won't give him a mouth. He doesn't need it for her to know that he's smiling.

She leans in to inhale his scent. It has faded, but not altogether. Some of him still mixes with the air. Parting her lips, she blows on him, lightly.

A small spot of sugar dances away, tickled by her breath. It teases her. Dares her to follow. Instead, she sweeps back the hem of her dress, runs her finger along an oozing dribble of cream, and rubs what comes on her naked thigh. It is sticky, and catches on her skin.
    The cake's right eye glints, coyly.
    If the others had had their way he would have been a chocolate sponge, drowning in messy, melting clumps. Not his style, she argued. This is what he would have wanted.

    The doorbell rings. That will be them. She is tempted not to answer, but fears the repercussions. Standing, she smoothes down her hem. She plucks out a berry and swallows it hastily, looking at him with tender eyes.
    'That'll be your kids,' she says. 'Coming to claim their piece of you.'
    She snorts at her joke.
    Before she opens the door, she picks up the urn and empties the remains into a kitchen jar. There's plenty left, thank goodness.
    She won't share him, next time.

Martin, Michelle and Diane

Martin sits at the kitchen table, his feet in brown brogues, legs crossed at the shins. 'I need to go away,' he says.
    'Again?' Michelle stops buttering the bread and looks at him. He's reading the newspaper. 'Where is it this time?' she asks.
    He finishes his paragraph and looks back at her. 'Wolverhampton.' He picks up the coffee she has made him. 'I'm meeting an associate.'
    Michelle takes some cheese from the fridge and starts to slice it. 'Not too thick,' says Martin. 'You know I don't like it when there's too much cheese.'
    She narrows the gaps with her knife. 'That good enough for you?'
    'Yes, thanks,' he says. 'That's perfect.' As he reads, Michelle layers the cheddar on to the bread and presses his lunch together.
    When he gets to the end of the page, he holds it, steadily, before his face. 'Would you like me to invite Diane?' he asks. Michelle does not

answer immediately. Instead, she opens a blue Tupperware box, places the sandwiches inside, and reaches for an apple from the fruit bowl.

'I don't like it when she comes to visit,' she says.

'Why?'

'She takes control of everything.' The apple is rinsed in cold water.

'She doesn't,' he says.

'Yes, Martin. She does.'

He lays the paper before him, exhales, and plays with the side of the table. 'It's too late now,' he says. 'She's coming anyway.' Michelle rolls her eyes and seals the Tupperware lid. She leaves the kitchen, wiping her hands on her jeans. At the bottom of the stairs she rests her palm on the wall. 'Robbie,' she shouts. 'It's time for school.'

Martin gets ready to go.

Diane arrives late in the afternoon. Martin has left.

When the doorbell rings, Michelle is painting her fingernails fuchsia. She does not stop what she is doing: she still has three more nails to go. They are all on her right hand – a difficult side to paint properly. The doorbell rings for a second time. One nail is left. She paints it slowly and carefully – none of it gets to the skin. She blows on the varnish and shakes out her hands. The bracelets on her arm clink lightly.

Diane tries knocking. No answer. She pushes the letterbox inwards. 'Hello?'

When Michelle opens the door they stand face to face. Diane hugs her, pinning her arms to her sides.

'Careful of my nails,' she says.

Michelle is followed to the kitchen, where she sits down and picks up a magazine. Diane turns on the kettle. She gets the teapot and two mugs, puts teabags inside, and pours milk into a jug. 'How have you been?' she asks, smiling.

'Fine,' says Michelle.

They wait. The kettle boils, steam wetting the window. 'Is Robbie upstairs?' Diane asks, putting the things on a tray.

'He's out.'

Diane frowns. 'I hoped he would be in,' she says. 'Martin told him I was coming.'

'He didn't want to stay,' says Michelle. Diane sets down the tray and sits on the opposite chair.

'When is he back?'

'Sometime in the morning.'

'The morning? Is that a good idea?' Michelle lowers her magazine and glares. 'OK,' says Diane. 'Fine.' She pours out the tea and pushes a mug across the table. She points at Michelle's nails. 'I like the colour,' she says. 'It suits you.'

'Thanks.'

'How do you do them so neatly? I always end up painting my fingers.' Diane laughs. 'I guess I need more practice.'

'I guess you do,' Michelle replies. She watches as Diane smoothes down her skirt. It is covered in violet flowers. 'That looks familiar,' she says.

'One of your cast-offs, I believe. Like it?'

'Hmm.' Michelle goes to the wine rack, selecting a green-labelled bottle. It is a screw-cap. She undoes it, grabs a glass from the cupboard and fills it up halfway. After a heavy swig, she redoes the cap and leans against the kitchen worktop. 'I'm going out as well,' she says. 'You're on your own this evening.'

'What?'

'You heard.'

'Martin didn't mention –'

'Martin didn't know.'

'Well, what am I supposed to do?' asks Diane. 'I thought we could have dinner together. Watch a film.'

'You know where the DVDs are.'

Diane tenses. Her veins make ridges on the backs of her hands. Her nostrils whistle. 'Where are you going?' she asks.

'To dinner.'

'With who?'

'A friend.'

'Anyone I know?'

'No. You don't know him.'

'Him?' Diane says, her voice rising. 'What would Martin say?'

'I have no idea,' Michelle replies. 'Perhaps, if he were around more, I

Georgie Codd

would.' She takes another swig. Her lips are turning purple, their cracks darkening.

Diane stands up and walks over to the sideboard. Her forehead is creased. She looks at the floor. 'It's not his fault,' she says, her voice deep and tired. 'He can't help it if he has to leave.'

'Really?'

'Really.'

'He's told you that, has he?' Michelle says, fiercely.

'Yes.'

'But why does he have to leave, Diane? I don't understand it myself.'

Diane thinks. 'For – for the family.'

'The family? How's that?'

'To make it easier. For everyone.'

'Ha!' Michelle slams down her glass. A wave of wine leaps out and splashes onto the floor. She leaves the kitchen and goes up to her bedroom. The door slams.

Later, they hear a car parking outside. Michelle runs downstairs immediately, reaching the door before Diane is even in the hallway. She pulls on her coat. Diane stiffens, waiting for explanations. There are none.

'Goodbye, Diane,' says Michelle. She leaves without shutting the door. Diane rests her back on the wall and fiddles absent-mindedly with her ring.

Michelle has not said when she'll return, so Diane gets the varnish from her dressing table and tries to paint her nails. She cannot keep her hands still enough to do it properly. Streaks of fuchsia trail up her fingers. She finds cotton wool pads but not the varnish remover. Bits of fluff cling to her skin.

She opens Michelle's wardrobe and pulls out a long, black satin dress. The neckline is studded with glass beads and sequins. She takes off her clothes and tries it on. The fabric clings round her middle and the zip won't go up all the way. Facing the mirror, it is more difficult to tell that it doesn't fit. A broad, lacy shawl from the back of the door will cover up the problem.

'Hello,' she says to the mirror. Her lip curls up, suggestively. She tilts her head forward and looks at herself from beneath her eyelashes. 'Have

we met before?' She gathers the folds of the dress and curtseys, allowing her shoes to peek out. Her other clothes are crumpled on the bed. She moves them to one side and lies back on the duvet cover. Her eyes shut. Her breathing is heavy.

Diane is in the kitchen when Michelle arrives home. It is almost lunchtime, the next day. Michelle's make-up is smeared, her eyes a dark brown smudge. She unbuttons her cardigan and throws it to the floor. Diane sits at the table.
'You're wearing my dress,' says Michelle as she enters.
Diane is solemn. 'Did you spent the night with him?' she asks.
'What gives you the right to take my clothes?'
'What gives you the right to be with other men? You're married.'
'And so are you.' Michelle is flushed in pink.
'I've never cheated.'
'No,' Michelle replies. 'You've done much worse.' There is a pause. Diane scratches the table with her fingernail. 'I want a divorce,' says Michelle.
'What?'
'I've had enough.'
'But –'
'But nothing. Where's Martin?'
'He's away. You know –'
'Stop messing me around, Diane.' Michelle inspects her nails, then continues. 'Put your own clothes on. You look ridiculous. You always do.'
Diane stands up and lifts her hair. Without the wig her head is almost bald.
'There,' she says. The voice drops. 'Happy?' He unwraps the shawl from his shoulders and peels off the dress. He is wearing women's lingerie. Beige.
'How could you?' he says. 'Another man?'
'The only man.'
Martin sighs. 'I'm still your husband.'
'And what about Diane?'
He eyes the dress on the floor. 'She's gone now,' he says.
'Oh really?' says Michelle. She looks at his underwear. Her mouth

clamps shut in disgust.

'I thought you understood,' he says.

She scoffs at his remark. 'Nobody understands,' she says. 'I thought I was marrying *you.*'

'Can't you try to love us both?'

Michelle thinks about this. She looks out of the window. 'I don't love either of you anymore,' she says. 'Now get out, before Robbie comes home.'

Martin's eyes start filling. The tears seep onto his lashes, mingling with his mascara.

He picks the clothes up off the floor. And leaves.

Georgie Codd was the winner of last year's Seth Donaldson Memorial Bursary. Now 23, her previous work – at a funeral parlour, newspaper and Tibetan nunnery – continues to influence her writing. Though a fan of flash fiction, her current project is a novel of exchanges, set between the desert and Dorchester.

Gordon Collins

Professional Dysfunction Syndrome
Chapter One of a novel

The Impossibility of Farming

I sit in a puddle in the north field and I sigh. Oh, I've been a terrible farmer since Father died. I've got the pigs in the trees while the apples go to slaughter. I've been ploughing the haystacks and sowing the chickens. I harvest the tractors and take the barn to market. I'm not cut out for this.

I wish Father had written something down for me. Just a few lines about how to farm – which field the sheep go into, how to spread the muck, when to shear parsnips – but he hardly told me anything. In fact, he hardly ever spoke to me. He'd just tut or sigh as he watched my pathetic attempts at agriculture. Now I can't remember if it's the potatoes or the plough that needs milking.

The one piece of advice he did give me was to get a good wife. 'Gawd's sake, son, get thee good wife,' he'd say. He'd say it almost every day and I suppose I should be thankful for that because I did marry well. I got a real beauty, 'a good 'un,' he would have said. Attentive, loving and sensible too – just the kind he wanted for me. I've got her planted in the south field. I reckon I'll get two tonnes off her when she's ripe.

Maybe that's because it's sunnier there in the south field. Here in the north field, the chickens aren't growing so well. I planted them neatly in rows but I didn't know which way up to put them so I did some head first and some feet first. None of them have grown much. In fact some of them have escaped and are running all over the place and they're the ones that look the most edible.

Edibility is the main goal of farming, you see. That's one thing I've learnt here. You can have all the latest theories, all the resource management systems, and read all the farming journals but if your product's not edible the supermarkets aren't going to touch it. Edibility is one of those things they probably don't emphasise enough at college but which, 'in the real world', is actually very important.

Of course there's a place for agricultural colleges. I'd be the first to say that. I went to the new university here in Juxton. I went there thinking farming was just a matter of feeding animals and planting crops and nothing more complicated than that. Well, they soon changed my mind on that score. I studied 'Bovine Meta-Semantics', 'Issues in Ruminant Theory', 'Reconstructing the Farm-Farm Dialectic in the Wake of the Goat Paradox' and my practical module was 'Pigs. Pigs?' taught by Professor Jean Verbenez – perhaps the world's most renowned agri-philospher.

What an interesting man he was. He'd lived all over the world and spoke seven languages. He'd studied economics, art history, biochemistry and philosophy at some of the best universities in Europe. He'd done a PhD in the 'Philosophy of Socialised Digestibles' and gone on to join Metzier's Paris group. For a while he was one of the key figures in the anti-farming movement although he eventually came to reject Metzier's doctrine, 'Ce n'est pas une vache. C'est une désaccord d'alimentation' – 'It is not a cow. It is a food conflict'. Instead Professor Verbenez took the debate a step further. He argued against all food. In effect he saw the conflict had been won by the animals. I remember him telling us. 'See the horse boxes behind the cars? Only one hundred years before, the horse it was transporting us, and now?' and he would shrug his shoulders for up to five minutes ignoring all our questions. He more or less discounted the very possibility of farming. 'What is the pig? What is the pig?' he would ask and, when none of us could answer, 'Voila! There is no pig,' he'd exclaim. He didn't see any value in food or farming beyond the aesthetic value. He deconstructed the farm as, 'The contingent relations between agricultural atoms'. 'Why butcher the pig? Why plough the field? We may as well plough the pig and butcher the field,' he told us. Although I may have got that all the wrong way around.

After three years studying agriculture I thought I knew all about farming, but when I started back here … well, talk about the gap

between theory and practice! I came back with my head filled with theories. I was sure I knew how a farm should be run. I really thought I had something to teach Father. I gave him Professor Verbenez's papers. I told him about the pigs. I tried to open his mind to things beyond farming and the production of food. 'There are alternative agricultural discourses,' I told him.

I suppose I was naïve. You can't run a farm that way and Father knew it. The divide between us became clear when, only a week after my return from college, Father assigned me a simple muck-spreading task. I decided to employ a technique I had recently read about in 'New Farming Now'. Instead of haphazardly spreading muck around a field, I pumped balloons full of it and placed them around the farm. Methane would build up and eventually burst the balloon and spread its contents. The gaudy balloons' shocking disintegration into stinking primal sludge would be the perfect demonstration of our foolish attempts to engineer nature. At the same time, the muck would be spread in an efficient manner that I thought Father would appreciate.

He didn't see it that way. In fact he made it clear I wasn't to help on the farm any more. Instead I was to concentrate on the courting and marriage of a good farmer's wife. 'Pref'ably with some sense 'cos thou's got none,' he told me. I'd had some interest from those girls who hang around The Pig and Whistle looking for a young farmer but I wasn't ready for marriage. I suppose I still thought I could impress him with my farming and so I stayed in my room, reading the latest journals, corresponding with my classmates and learning about their radical projects. I spent hours poring over the glossy farming magazines and dreaming that one day I would be on the cover like Lambert or Verbenez posing in front of their latest creations – the carrot carousel or the well of sheep. I drew my own designs for how we could transform the farm – a giant pig with ploughs racing across its back, grain flowing from its snout and honey streaming from its teats or multi-storeyed fig farms or sausages rolling along roads of bacon spreading out across the county or vegetables oscillating on a system of springs and thus making manifest Coulthard's 'Adaptive Farming Domains'.

But then, only a year before I met my wife, Father died. I took over the farm and I had to be a bit more realistic about what is achievable. I still have ambitions but they are tempered by the realities of everyday

farming and the reality is that edibility is paramount. Unfortunately edibility is the weakest aspect of my farming. Still, with the example of my father to aspire to and the education I have had, I like to think I've got the best of both worlds. Most of the time I'm thinking, 'What would Father do?' but often I go back to my old lecture notes to check up on things like how to use an arable.

It's no good sitting here in a pile of mud. I crawl out of the puddle, stand up and clean myself up as best I can. I found a couple of turnips today. They might be edible. I'll take them to my wife to see what she thinks.

But as I set off, I hear a branch snap. I jump out of the way of a pig as it falls off the tree and hits the ground with a sort of grunting sound. I examine its thin crumpled body embedded in the mud. It doesn't look ripe enough. Oh dear.

I carefully step between the chickens who try to peck my ankles. I'm glad to leave the north field but then, as I climb the stile, I can see the mess which is my experimental turnip field. It has neither productive nor aesthetic value, even in a progressive sense. It all smells rotten. Luckily, though, I can see my neighbour Mr Clive coming from the south field. He's good at turnips. I'll ask him for advice.

'Ahhhh,' I call out to him, colloquially.

'All right,' he calls back. His hands are deep in his tracksuit pockets as he takes long strides across my field. He's grinning – he is happy on the land. That's something I could learn from. I tend to run around in a panic.

We converge at one of the gates that I have put around the farm. I lean on it, say, 'Ahhh,' again, and gesture to the vacant gate space.

'Ah,' he replies. He rather barks it, though. But then he looks me in the eye, resumes his grinning and leans onto the gate next to me.

We're silent for a while. Or perhaps I should say we let the farm speak first. It's a sunny, only slightly crisp autumn late afternoon. We look northeast across my turnip field and down to the copse on Mr Clive's land. We can hear the rustle of leaves with each sway of the breeze and with each rustle a few leaves fall. Some birds look like they might head south soon. The air has a richer smell than in summer. The sunlight is weaker too. The puddles dotted around my field sparkle only occasionally. Behind us the carrots are lowing.

We're silent. Actually, this is good farming discourse. Agricultural discourse is rarely conducted face to face but is better done facing the farm. In that way it's more of a three-way discourse which reflects the farm-farmer-farmer trialectic. It makes sense.

Mr Clive's father was my father's best friend. They'd spend hours together leaning on one particular rotten old gate up on the north field, on the border between the farms. When I took over here, I was keen to make use of Mr Clive's expertise and so I had gates built all over the farm. These are agricultural discourse gates, though. They're positioned for optimal views of the fields and they've got padded leather patches to rest your arms on. I'm pleased to say they have been successful and the farm gate tradition has continued from fathers to sons. It's probably been my best bit of farming.

"Tatoes gawn rotten in top field,' he eventually says.

'That'll be needing some muck then,' I say informedly. It's a sort of catch-all.

He nods.

Actually, I'm rather pleased with that. I could say something more about Verbenez's theory of muck transference but I think it's best not to. Clive didn't go to university and, while I accept that he is more experienced than me, I find he is not very open to the theories I have occasionally tried to bring to our gate talks. He produces a lot of edible crop – turnips especially – but it's just that sometimes his farming seems too simplistic.

Still, we have a good discourse. I learn a lot from these sessions. I'm going to do another 'Ahhh', wait for a while and then ask him something about turnips.

But instead he says, 'See your wife's set in south field,' and he grins broadly.

'Oh yes, she's a good wife isn't she? A good 'un, I mean. As you know my father always said that I should get a good wife and I don't think he could argue ...'

'She won't be needin' fertilisin' today,' he says, adjusting his trousers and walking off.

Gordon Collins (www.zipple.co.uk) has been a mathematician, a market risk analyst, a computer graphics researcher and a teacher. He has been published in *Riptide – Vol. 3* and *Danse Macabre*.

Maire Cooney

Nobody Said Anything
Extract from a novel

JANICE

23:55

Nearly there

23:56

The trick is to keep your eyes fixed

23:57

on the green glowing numbers. They float. They slip and slide if you aren't careful. But if you watch they change. Time moves on. And so I wait. Today can end, it always does. You just have to wait

23:58

wait

23:57

It does that sometimes. I wasn't careful enough. I lost focus.

23:58

Before all this, time moved approximately in ways I understood. It would speed, slow, depending on what was going on. It passed in ways I found surprising but mainly enjoyable. A new month, a year, faster than days. It was life and it was fine.

23:58

And then it stopped moving forward at all. Moments like months, and days like days I've been through before. It stalls, it stops, sometimes it slips back and I have to live it all over again. I have to Take Each Day At A Time. I have to Allow Myself To Remember. And this is fine. I'm not averse to allowing myself anything. More tricky is Dr Roberts's advice, Let Time Heal. Old-fashioned, he said, and true. But it's hard. I lose concentration and time slips back.

23:54

The tablets help of course. I am to Take As Directed. Dr Philips was usefully indirect. When you need to sleep, he said, when you need a rest. Negligent possibly, or the kindest man I know. But they don't make me sleep, or rest. What they do, I've discovered, is work on time. Little white pills that daze, cotton-wool the body and muffle the mind. Nice enough but not enough. They work better in twos and threes. Dr Philips is vague enough with dates and repeat prescriptions to make this possible, and him my favourite at that particular practice.

23:55

I go to two practices. One day they'll realise this, but time isn't what it was and so I can't be sure that day will ever arrive. Meanwhile the tablets help

23:56

move time forward.

23:57

Some days they sledgehammer time – smash it to pieces.

00:11

There

00:12

A new day

00:15

There's a limit to what medicine can do, naturally. There's no such thing as a magic pill. There's also a maximum daily dose. Sensible, in the usual way of things, but days aren't days any more and so a maximum daily dose is meaningless. I'm left to improvise. But I'm not stupid, not one for melodrama. I stay approximately within my own limits.

00:05

Though limits can be frightening. I need to get safely into the next day and stay there. It isn't easy. No magic pills, but there are magic cocktails. I mixed one earlier and it should be working its magic, any hour, any minute now. Vodka and Valium. I really hit on something there.

00:07

It helps things along. Time is more my own now. A new day dawns and this one is not an anniversary, not by any standards. I am not allowed to make it one, Dr Roberts's advice. It's too easy to make anniversaries of days, weeks, months. A year. A year was supposed to do something helpful – the turning of the seasons, a new start. But on and on it goes.

00:09

I am not to blame. Many people have said this and so it must be true. I am not to blame. This seems true, it may actually be true, but the alternative You Are To Blame is unlikely to be used by any health care professional, which must make their truth unreliable at best. There has to be someone to blame and God knows I've tried to make it someone else.

00:11

There is no one else.

00:17

We never bothered much, me and Michael. I don't doubt he hates me drinking. In the old days, in real life, he would have suggested it was weak, selfish even, but of course he can't say anything now, not since it happened. Just enough to muddle the senses. Nothing wrong with that.

00:22

But then

00:29

Vodka with the weekly shop. The bottle lying flat in the Co-op trolley with the cornflakes, tins and milk. The woman rolling it and packing it and not a word. Enough reason to stop. Until the next night, lying worn-awake, thoughts sharp and burning and the birds outside the window, screaming like witches on helium, a squabbling racket, the sun coming up and no rest, not a bit of sleep and the whole day to manage again and again and just a splash of vodka, a mouthful to slow it all down. That was enough.

00:37

Coping. That was the word Dr Roberts used, which sounds alarming, desperate, though I'm sure he didn't mean it to. Coping well, he'd said, but perhaps a little time off might be wise? A sensible idea, because crying while dressing ulcers and putting in eye drops can be difficult, alarming for the patients. People like their nurses no-nonsense. So I took time off, and time stopped, and so I went back. No nonsense. I have a job to do. For Ewan especially, because he can't remember and so he can't understand. I am a good mother. I tell him all the right things.

00:43

Told him all the right things.

00:48

There is nothing to say now.

01:05

I did not mention God, though Michael believes in God and so perhaps I should try.

01:12

Does he still believe? I have no idea. I hope he does. He believed in a lot of things.

01:17

Another few should see me through.

01:33

Work in the morning.

01:49

I work

02:09

I am a good nurse

02:16

May sleep, may not, doesn't matter either way

02:37

No point to days but they keep coming. I have responsibilities. I remember

MICHAEL

It was something to do with stillness. I see that clearly now, standing at the kitchen door, peering into the thick black. Something inside me is wrong. Nothing hurt, but a friction, an abrasion, something of that sort, inside my chest. There is a sander in there, working away days and nights. I am being hollowed out, it seems, worn to nothing, but it's here, in these few hours before dawn, that something repairs inside and I am solid again.

And so here I am, ten to five in the morning, eating a bread and butter sandwich, drinking a mug of sweet tea. I didn't make toast, the smell of toast would wake them, perhaps. I dressed quietly, came down and buttered bread, made tea. I do this often but today I have the best of all reasons. Work. Up in the cold dark, getting ready for work. The way I used to work, years ago.

I butter another two slices and then I get up, look in the cupboard and find some jam. A jam piece. That makes me smile, a piece and jam. I eat happily for a moment and then I get up and walk through.

I push the living room door quietly. The TV is on, the white and grey

dots spinning silently, and Jan is on the sofa, lying on her side, her head on one arm. She looks uncomfortable lying that way, and yet I know she is sleeping too heavily to register any discomfort, or to change position. I do not know how to help her. She won't talk about this, about any of it. I pull the door over and stand there, my forehead on the door, my eyes closed, the friction burning, grinding my ribcage, and then I open the door again, go quickly across and bend and kiss her. She frowns, shakes her head slightly. The smell of vodka is not a surprise but it's shocking just the same. I smooth her hair down, put a hand on her cheek and leave it there, just for a minute.

There's a draught blowing on the landing and I remember now, leaving the loft door open to remind me to put the box up. I had time when Janice was out yesterday, plenty of time and I had forgotten to do it. Forgotten because I did not want to do it and because it is necessary and final. I do not want to think about it.

There's a square of dark where the loft door should be. Ewan will have been frightened of the loft being open, of ghosts and monsters up there. He will have run from the bedroom to the bathroom with his hands on top of his head. I should close it over. I should do what I failed to do yesterday, and then shut the loft door over.

The box is behind the door in the boy's room. I lift it up and glance round. It is freezing in here, the coldest room in the house, but it's colder then it should be. The curtain is blowing, the bottom of it sucking in and out. I go over and pull the window down, my fingertips burning with the black cold. I can't imagine why they've left it open. Ewan is at the bottom of his bed, the blankets half off, curled tight under the sheet, his hands up under his chin, legs tucked into his belly. I pull the blankets back onto the bed and tuck them round him. He is holding something in his fist. A hanky, with dark spots on it and I remember his tooth, another one loose, and I smile. He has been trying to pull it out.

I hear a creaking behind me. Jamie, awake and up on one elbow, watching me. I nod across to him. He sits up, pulls his covers round him, shivering.

What you doing? he says. Did you open a window? I shake my head. He looks over at the box. Are you putting it up in the loft? he says.

I sit down on the edge of his bed. Do you want me to put it up? I say.

His shoulders drop. I don't know, he says. What are you asking me for?
I'll put it in the loft, I say.
He lies down, hands behind his head. All right, he says.

I put the box on the landing and swing up onto the stairs. Then I reach up into the loft, grab the edge of the ladder, pull it forward and down. It drops quietly. I lift the box onto the ladder and climb up, pushing the box ahead of me and into the loft. I keep a hold of it. I do not want to put it down, here, in the dark. My fingers touch the Sellotape on the edge and I have an urge to pull it off, to lift out the things I know are in there and bring them back down and into the house. I know each thing in there. And I stand, my head and shoulders in the loft, feet on the ladder and holding the box. I feel a sobbing pushing up and into my throat, my eyes burning and I need to scream, to howl, but I will not cry out. I take a few deep breaths and I push the box across the planks until it hits something and won't slide any further. I pull a dustsheet across and over it, cover it as best I can, although I'm shaking and can't manage it well. Then I climb back onto the top of the stairs and push the ladder up. I am still young enough to do this though Jan thinks I should use a chair, that I will hurt myself, that the children will copy me and also hurt themselves. She has not said any such thing, of course, but it seems the sort of thing she should have said. She used to tell me things like this.

Maire Cooney was born in Edinburgh and lives in London with her partner and two children.

Edward Dadswell

Hunger
An extract from a short story, set in Ukraine

Andriy looked at the bed, curving above him like a great hill. He could see from the slow swelling and falling of the covers that his grandfather Olek was still asleep. At the foot of the bed stood a circle of tiny figures: knights, soldiers, and assorted animals. Andriy sat down cross-legged in front of them. He began playing a game in which one of the knights had just chosen a new horse, whom he could ride into battle whenever there were enemies to be slain.

'You are a warhorse now, Hryhoriy,' he said (for this was the horse's name). 'Your work will be hard and you will not have oats whenever you please.'

Hryhoriy neighed a couple of times to show he understood the seriousness of his task. Before Andriy could continue with the story, however, there was a cry from the bed and his grandfather awoke.

The old man turned over, looking at Andriy from beneath lowered eyelids. He held out his arms and Andriy walked up to him.

'You can't imagine it,' he said, taking Andriy's face in his hands. 'Such hunger. You can't imagine.' He ran his thumbs over Andriy's eyebrows, peering closely into his eyes as if to see whether Andriy could imagine it or not.

He let go and rolled onto his back, but went on talking.

'Viktor Stasiuk had the finest pair of hunting dogs you ever saw. Used to walk with them through the village every Sunday to visit his daughter and son-in-law, and home again at night. My father would look at those dogs and ask him, "Eh, Viktor, what will you take for the pair?" And

Viktor would answer him: "For these fine beasts? Ten chervintsi and your wife – I'll accept nothing less."'
Andriy's grandfather paused for a moment, swallowing loudly.
'That always used to make Papa smile. "So," he would say, "you'll give me the dogs and take my wife off my hands, and all you want for your trouble is ten chervintsi? No, Viktor, I couldn't let a friend of mine make such a poor deal for himself!"'
Andriy's grandfather gave a dry chuckle that quickly turned into a fit of coughing. Andriy watched him, not knowing what he should do, but at length the coughing subsided and his grandfather continued speaking.
'Viktor went on walking past with his dogs, even when he had to sell his best coat and boots to buy bread with. Awful bony creatures they were, then. None of us had enough food. He and Papa didn't know what to say to each other any more – often Papa would go inside and shut the door when he saw Viktor coming along the road. By the time Viktor had the heart to kill his dogs, there was barely enough flesh on them to make it worthwhile. And after that, I think he was too ashamed to go walking through the village. We didn't see him again.'
Andriy's grandfather looked at the ceiling as a tear slid from the corner of his eye. Then he said: 'And there was a crow, once.'
Andriy climbed onto the bed and lay down beside him, hoping for another story.
'Oh, he was a wise one.' Andriy's grandfather smiled at the thought. He had enjoyed watching this crow as it went about its business: cawing from the chestnut tree or raking the ground for seeds, or dropping snails in the yard until their shells broke. When the hunger began to wear away at them, he and his brother Ivan made a plan to catch this bird.
One morning they crept into the garden and began digging, gouging up clods of damp earth with their hands. Whenever they found an earthworm they dropped it into a bucket and went on with their work. The effort made them feel faint, so that everything they looked at seemed to boil in black and gold.
When they had enough worms, Olek took the bucket onto the front path where he could see the crow sitting in its usual place in the chestnut tree. He threw a worm onto the path and backed away while he

waited for the crow to notice. At last it flew down a small distance away and spent several moments watching Olek. It turned its head and looked at him with one eye, made a feint at taking the worm and then drew back to give him another sideways look. A grey translucent eyelid flashed across the black of its eye. When the crow had judged it was safe to proceed, it lunged for the worm and flapped backwards a couple of steps to eat. Olek waited until it had almost finished and carefully threw another worm onto the path. When it had eaten that one, he threw another. While this was going on, Ivan emerged from behind the woodshed with a sack and began making his way with long, silent strides towards the crow. Olek prayed it would not turn its head. When Ivan was about three feet away he darted forward, but the crow saw what was happening and tried to take off, so that Ivan only managed to pin half its body under the edge of the sack. Just as it pulled itself free, Ivan caught hold of its wing. The bird began flapping frenziedly and Ivan was shouting at Olek, 'Wring its neck! Wring its neck!', but Olek was afraid of this mass of thrashing claws and feathers, and horrified at the idea of taking its warm, pulsing neck in his hands and twisting it.

'Olek!' Ivan shouted once more, cuffing his brother round the head with his free hand. But Olek just stood there, until Ivan finally crushed the wing tightly in his fist and brought the crow's body down onto the path four times with all his strength, by which time the bird was sufficiently stunned that he could take its neck in both hands and break it himself.

The exertion had worn him out and he knelt there gasping for several moments, looking at Olek for a long time but saying nothing. The crow lay in front of them with its eyes tight closed, feathers softly parted at the back of the neck, claws curled up as if in ecstasy.

When Ivan had recovered his breath, he picked the crow up by its feet and they took it indoors to their mother. She made her way slowly to the front step and began plucking out its feathers with no expression on her face. Afterwards she put it in the oven, and the fumes of roasting crow made them all feel light-headed. When it was served up there was nothing to go with it, but it was strange how a few dark crescents of flesh could seem so much like a feast. Ivan and Olek were celebrated as heroes for outwitting the crow, and the family drew their lips over their

teeth in approving smiles. They might have laughed if it hadn't felt so much like their ribs would break.

The following day his mother took the crow's bones and boiled them to make a soup, and then his father ground them up and used them to eke out the last of the flour.

This was what Andriy's grandfather meant when he said there had been a crow. But the words fell brokenly from his mouth, and Andriy only understood the gist of the story. He felt sorry for his grandfather, but also felt some pity for the crow. Crows were meant to be the clever ones in stories, and didn't usually end up being eaten. No animal in a story usually got eaten unless it was particularly vain or stupid, and then it probably deserved it.

Andriy thought for a while and then said, 'Why didn't you have any food?'

'It was taken away, Andriy. The Party said the farmers weren't producing enough grain. They thought we were keeping some of it back. All of us were starving, and they thought we had hidden our grain!' He shook his head. 'After it was collected, most of it was locked up and left to rot. We knew people who were shot for trying to break into the grain stores. We were told it was all needed in case of an emergency. It wasn't an emergency that half the country was starving to death.'

Andriy looked at the pattern on the bedcovers. There was a loose thread in his hands that he kept twisting and twisting, but he said nothing.

'In the end, Mama and I were the only ones left.' The old man's voice had hardly any force left in it, and his speech was full of pauses. 'That last day, she told me we would go for a walk.'

Olek could still see her, stood in the kitchen, as she said this. She had made a fold in the side of her dress and tied it at the waist with a strip of fabric, so it wouldn't hang so loosely. Her face seemed almost worn away.

He couldn't understand why she had made this suggestion. The idea seemed almost frivolous – as if she'd somehow forgotten that his father, his brother, his sisters, were all dead.

'Where would we go?' he asked.

Edward Dadswell

'To Odessa.'

Her words made no sense. How could they walk to Odessa, when they could barely stand? Olek had only a vague idea of how far it was, but he had never heard of anyone going there on foot. He felt as if the room didn't have enough air in it, yet his head seemed full of the stuff. It was impossible to keep hold of his thoughts. He couldn't even feel surprise at what his mother said – it was simply nonsense. But then she pulled a threadbare coat around his shoulders and threw open the door. The world yawned out in front of them. Olek stood on the front step and the pale sunlight stung his eyes.

Then they began walking. Olek knew they wouldn't be able to go far, so he humoured his mother and went after her. But she didn't stop. He looked back at the house, wondering if they would return, but felt no regret at leaving. It was just another place now, and they were going somewhere else. From then on, he kept his eyes on the road.

Olek's mother said they must hide if they saw anyone, but the way was deserted. They heard a truck only once, and she dragged him into some bushes where the branches caught at their hands and clothes. The rest of the time she hardly let him stop for breath, and when she did, she said they had to stay on their feet. It didn't matter what they felt, they had to keep going.

Half a mile outside the city, it was Olek's mother who began to falter. Pausing every few steps and clutching her side, she finally sank onto the road. Olek was going to lie down with her but she held him up and said, 'No.' He'd never seen such a look of want in her face. She drew him towards her and said quietly, 'You'll go on without me.'

Olek pulled away. 'I'm not going to leave you!'

'You are, or I'll give you a hiding like you won't believe.' Her voice shook as she said it.

She took hold of him again and held him close to her; shoulders and chins pressing sharply together. He could feel her thinness, and his own. She kissed him and held him at arm's length and told him he had to keep going. Then she made him turn around and pushed him in the direction of the city, and Olek went on walking.

Edward Dadswell had a misspent youth studying physics, before deciding to be sensible and become a writer. He has worked mainly on short stories, but is currently writing a novel. He lives in a garret in London.

Anna Delany

What You Will Receive
An extract from the opening of a novel

What You Will Receive

But you know, don't you? Sitting there in a hard-backed chair reading your battered Shakespeare by candlelight, while your household sleeps – at least this night – in peace, that I'm going to get this story wrong. I'll have a door where there was a window, a decision where there wasn't one, an argument where there were only kind words. And for that, Charles, I apologise. But I have to try.

1.

Buckinghamshire, 1888

The boy lies awake in the cold room with its blue walls, between clean, white sheets, the top one folded down over a heavy blanket that makes his arms itch if the sheet loses its place. The light in the room is dull, but outside, he imagines, bright summer clouds are racing along, puffed out, high in the blue sky. Or perhaps there are low clouds today, grey and scratchy like his blanket. Or maybe, as usual, the sky is white and sunless. All this he thinks in a few blissful seconds, before he remembers the bruise on his arm – a plum-coloured smear now, threaded with red lines – and the face of the woman who put it there and who is right now coming up the stairs. Her hard little shoes, black and shining – she spits on them to get them to shine, he's seen her do it – make a clopping sound as they

approach, and as the sound gets louder he begins to sweat.

'Mother,' he whispers into the warm sheet. 'Mother, Mother, Mother.'

She is not his mother, but Charles is to call her that. Mother is the name for the lady who goes with Father. There were two other Mothers before this one. He remembers Mother-Before, soft and kind and laughing, and saying his muddy knees were fine: 'Aren't they fine?! Boys' knees! Made for mud!' And his father smiling when she said this and other things as well. And before that, before he started to have an age, which was at first three, he remembers Mother with dark coarse hair and silver bits in it like ash, and a curling up, a gentle crushing, into her body that felt like his own but wasn't, and then he slaps his head with his hand because he is not to remember this. It is gone.

One floor below, Charles's father, Mr. Alfred James Wright, is in his bedroom talking to Baby Margaret in her cradle while he dresses for work. He is station master at Bletchley, Buckinghamshire, with three handsome children from his first marriage, two from the second, and one – rather too early – from the third, to his housekeeper. There won't be another. A pragmatic and gentle man, with a fondness for food and a large belly to show it, he coped with the loss of his first wife – his childhood sweetheart – from pneumonia, with humbling dignity. But the loss of his second – a kind soul who arrived like a dream and then was gone like one, the little infant with her – devastated him.

After months of sleeplessness and caring almost single-handedly for his children, whom he was determined would not suffer because of his suffering: putting food on the table, and clothes on their backs, and getting them off to bed and caring for their spiritual needs, and tending to their illnesses, and considering their educations, all the while working with absolute dedication the lines and bells and times and mechanics of the station, he became, finally, overwhelmed.

On a day spent seated in his bedroom chair, unable even to finish buttoning his shirt, his face stinking of wet tears, his children whispering at the doorway, and the train whistles stopped and the tracks jammed, and the carriages held up all over the South East, he settled the matter with himself. The next day, he paid a visit – tongue dry as stones – to an acquaintance and with a loan secured, sought the help of a live-in housekeeper.

She came, Mary-Jane, aged twenty-five, with scrubbed hands and face, a clean dress and thin blonde hair, her references commending her as reliable, trustworthy and hard-working, and her smile assuring him that his family would be taken good care of. He did catch a whiff then, of gin on the breath, but at that moment this, and her Anglicanism, seemed as weevils in the flour that could easily be picked out.

Across the room the boy sees the knob turn. He whispers 'Mother' once more. But when the door swings open and she is standing there in the arch of the doorway with her pale stringy hair and her morning gown, bearing a candle that is not needed, the words won't come. He forms the sounds in his mind, pictures them even, their fluid shapes, but he can't say them. *Good morning Mother. Good morning Mother.* It is what he is supposed to say, has been asked to say. If he does, it will be better for him and for everyone, and especially for Father. But he can't. She comes over to his bed then, and slowly, with one hand, pulls back the sheet and blanket. She pauses, gives him a look of exasperation – because of his 'insensitivities', that's what she calls it when he can't say 'Mother' – and then, calmly, without a sigh or a change in her expression, tips the dish holding the candle. The hot pooled wax pours out and onto his chest, burning.

Well, Charles. If I'm going to tell your story, you can hear mine, starting here, in this airport terminal where I'm in need of a shower. I've been wearing these same clothes forty hours now. Against my skin on the tube to Heathrow, on a plane to Hong Kong and then another to Sydney. They stink. The button at the waist of my jeans has pressed a hole into my stomach and I never want to wear this shirt again; the fabric has turned yellow under my armpits, which have grown a visible millimetre of hair. But it's still a five hour layover and one more flight until New Zealand, then an hour's drive to my mother's before I can change.

On the laptop in front of me is a scanned photo of you:
CHARLES WRIGHT, the typewritten caption says. **1911, CHRISTCHURCH HIGH STREET STUDIOS, NEW ZEALAND**. On my screen the photo is in sepia, but I can still see your blue eyes in the middle of it. They are a blue that has few counterparts in nature. Wash blue, pale blue, powder blue, a little ice blue. Your daughter, my great-aunt Vera, has the same eyes. My sister Sophie as well, but only the soul of them. Hers are green, in fact.

I wonder about your journey. Weeks on boats, shovelling coal hour after hour, day after day, across seas you barely saw except at night, when you came up from below deck, the whites of your eyes glowing and wet in the black dust that covered your face.

This airport terminal, with its whirly patterned carpet and hum of movement, could be anywhere. The coffee I'm drinking to try and knock myself into today tastes like transit coffee everywhere, slopped and dribbled down the anywhere paper cup onto the anywhere plastic table. When I look up though, out these windows at tarmac baking in morning sun, there's no mistaking this as the other side of the world. The sky is so damn blue. Did you notice it when you first arrived? Lyttelton harbour, New Zealand, 1910. Stepping from the deck over the seaweed-green sea to a jetty reeking of fish? A vast and empty blue, stretched out to the Southern Alps where rivers tumble down in a clack of stones and white water, ferns and beech trees, gorse and tussock, to the dry plains. Enough to make you stay.

2.

Washed, dressed, bed made. Charles is on the top stair when the breakfast gong sounds. On the second-floor landing below, Violet slips like a little gust of wind out of the girls' bedroom, late, like him. The gong is

a reprimand: they are expected to be there before it rings, and Mother rings it even if they are all there. Violet is tiny and Charles loves her. She looks like a doll but is more like a fox. She hides in corners and shadows so you don't even notice her, then suddenly – swoosh – she darts in front of you with her big brown eyes wide and says something extraordinary. Truly, sometimes he thinks maybe she is a nymph. Maybe she was born inside a flower and leapt out one day and ran away from the bees that might sting her and the birds that could snip her in half and hid in an empty fox hole until she grew big enough to be a baby for Mother-Before.

'Charles,' she whispers as he descends, pulling the mass of brown hair back from her face. 'We're late!' But her eyes tremble with excitement when she says it; she's not scared. It was only her six-year birthday last week and she is a girl so she won't get the telling-off. Though Mother is – what do they say? Full of surprises. Yes – but it's still likely him that'll get the blame for making Violet late. His young sister looks at him then tugs at his sleeve.

'Do you want to see my drawing?' she asks.

He wants to, but there goes the gonging again, louder this time.

'Please?'

Her eyes beg him into the bedroom and as she backs into it, he follows her. She goes to the chest of drawers, reaches up with her small arm, and pulls down a piece of paper.

'Look!'

He sees a fox with a bird in its mouth, a bed of crushed flowers under its feet. And in the corner of the page a little family of ants. One is wearing a hat. She beams at him. 'I did it myself.' It is good. It is excellent, in fact. Charles can't draw very well at all. And he is already eight.

They hear the black shiny shoes on the wooden stairs. Charles sucks in his breath and Violet bites her lip. Last night they hid her bottle, the one she keeps in the kitchen in the flour bin and that looks like water but isn't. Perhaps she's noticed already? But then comes the sound of heavier steps and a murmur in the stairwell.

'Violet? Charles!' It is Father who calls them, not Mother. Relief. The children emerge from the doorway to see him there on the first landing with his big belly and his whiskers that scratch like a brush when he kisses them and his watch on a chain hanging from his pocket. He gives them a

disapproving look as they rush down the stairs, but his eyes are not stern and the children are not scared.

'Don't run,' he says. They slow down. At the bottom of the stairs Violet holds her drawing up for him, her face transformed to solemn. Father accepts it and smiles down at her.

'It's very good Violet. Very good. I shall take it with me to the station today.' He looks at his son. 'Good morning Charles,' he says. Then he shepherds them both into the dining room, a hand on each of their backs.

Anna Delany's immediate project is this novel set in New Zealand, the UK and Saudi Arabia. She is also completing a collection of short stories about California and beginning a second about Finland. She has lived in each of these places.

Chelsey Flood

Silverweed
An extract from a novel

Chapter One

It was the end of our second summer without her when Mum rang.

The sky was the colour of a sucked-out blue ice-pop as I stood in the yard, hitting a ball with the coal scuttle for Fiasco, our dog. It flew over the pick-up that Dad was working on, over stripped-down cars and the abandoned chicken coop, over our vegetable patch and the tin foil pie-bottoms that dangled above it, and finally through our glassless greenhouse, to touch down behind the apple tree. Fiasco snatched it up as it bounced, and running across the home-made graves of her predecessors, dropped it at my feet.

'Last one,' I told her. Toeing the froth-covered ball onto the spade, I whacked it as hard as I could. Dog slobber landed on my face, and I ran into the kitchen. Dad walked in while I was wet-faced at the sink. He smelt of sweat and petrol and just-cut grass. Zombie-like, he held his filthy hands out towards me, and I ducked out of the way.

'Bloody pick-up,' he said, squeezing green soap onto his hands, and rubbing them together. Thick black grime dripped from his wrists onto the pots piled in the bowl. When he put the washing-up bottle back on the draining board there was a greasy hand print around its waist.

My big brother, Sam, popped his head round the door. 'What's for tea, Dad?'

Dad rubbed his right thumb into his left palm under the steaming tap, loosening the dirt. 'Crisps on toast?' he said.

This was Dad's idea of a joke. It meant he hadn't done the shopping. Sam never laughed.

'I'll make it,' I said, because Sam was still standing there. He went through to the living room, and put the telly on.

'I'll leave it with you then, Eye,' Dad said, drying his hands on a tea towel then wiping transferred cat fur onto his jeans. 'You're a better man than me.' He went upstairs to get changed.

I looked in the pantry: bread, pasta, crisps, pickled onions, tins. Dad bought tins even when we'd already got tins – baked beans, pineapple chunks, new potatoes – we were never short of these things. I opened a can of chicken soup and poured it into the biggest saucepan I could find, then sluiced mushroom soup in, using the tea left in the metal teapot on the back of the Aga to wash out the leftovers, like Dad did.

A few minutes later, Dad walked through the kitchen, tanned knees poking out of the holes in his faded jeans as he went, brown hair wild around his head. He opened the living room door and I heard David Attenborough say:

'... *from this vantage point, the lioness can scan, unobserved, miles of unforgiving ...*'

On the stove, bubbles emerged sluggishly from the mixture. I poured in a pack of spaghetti, forcing down the dry ends until they were covered, and went to sit down. Dad was in his green leather armchair by the unlit fire. Sam sat in the seat next to him, which was an itchy, floral thing that had belonged to Granny before she died.

Granny had been bird-boned with grey Rapunzel hair and tiny red shoes. She couldn't hear a thing. The telly bellowed at her while she squinted at her embroidery, occasionally stopping to shriek, 'Have I had my dinner?' In the end, Mum had started leaving her soup bowl on top of the telly so she could see when she'd had her dinner, but Nanny thought it was neglect.

'Nobody cares about me, Harry. That bowl's been there for weeks!'

I took the settee, which at night-time became Fiasco's bed. The living room floor was covered with wooden tiling. Years of dog and cat claws had scratched at the dark brown varnish, leaving lighter patches by the window sills and settee. Stuck to the ceiling, which like the walls was the texture and colour of rice pudding, was a mysterious dollop of tomato sauce.

Silverweed

On telly the lion stalked a gazelle.

'Oh no!' I couldn't help myself. 'It's got separated from its family.'

'From the herd, dickhead.'

'*Sam,*' Dad said.

The gazelle's eyes stared straight ahead, bow legs still trying to run away as the lion tore a chunk out of its throat. Settling down onto all fours, the lion's chest heaved sharp pants as it drained the blood from the gazelle's throat.

My brother looked at me holding my breath.

'You live in the countryside,' he said.

'That is correct,' I said. 'And dinner shall be served in five minutes.'

Back in the kitchen, the spaghetti was changing. If it wasn't soft yet, it was at least chewy. Everything was fine except that the meal was grey like the inside of a toilet roll. I tried to think of other foods that were grey like the inside of a toilet roll and I came up with pork.

'How's it going, Eye?' Dad said, looking over my shoulder.

'Pork is a grey food.'

'Does it taste all right?'

'Course,' I said, getting a teaspoon and tasting it for the first time. 'It tastes like chicken and mushroom soup.'

'What've you put in there?'

'Chicken and mushroom soup. And spaghetti.'

He held his hand out for the spoon.

'Mmm,' he said. 'Soupy!'

Sam leaned round the door frame from the living room. 'I'm meant to be meeting Benjy at seven.'

'It's ready.' Dad told him and I wanted to whoop because this was the closest he'd ever come to favouritism.

'Five minutes,' I said, making the most of it.

'Is that all you can say?'

'No, I can say dickhead as well. Dickhead.'

'*Iris,*' Dad said.

Sam went back into the living room and it became clear what the dish needed. Sweetcorn. I opened a can and shook some in.

'Maybe chilli powder too?' Dad said. I nodded and he sprinkled it on.

'It's no longer a grey meal,' I said, splitting a strand of spaghetti for us to try.

Dad slopped out three portions and, still keen to up the colour count, I added orange cheese.

The kitchen table stood in an alcove beneath a window decorated with different-sized muddy paw prints. It was surrounded on two sides by a low wooden storage chest that doubled as a bench. Dad took his usual seat opposite the window. With his back to the kitchen, he watched the birds outside. Sam and I sat at a right-angle to him, on the bench that was against the wall. I was closest to the window, Sam closest to Dad. Mum used to sit on the other wooden chair. Now Dad used it as a stop-off for clothes on their way to the line.

'This is disgusting,' Sam said, trawling through the grey and orange clag on his plate. He dropped a strand of spaghetti on the floor. 'Look. Even the dog won't eat it.'

'You are an ungrateful little sod sometimes, Sam. It's lovely, Iris. Thank you.'

The truth was somewhere between the two.

'Goldcrest on the aviary,' Dad said.

We all looked up. The aviary was a rotating washing line loaded with bird feeders and titbits. On it, a small gold-headed bird pecked at a piece of bacon rind.

When the phone rang Dad carried on eating. It was never for him after six o'clock.

'It's not going to be for me, is it?' Sam said.

'I'd love to answer it,' I said. 'But I can't get out.'

'Sam,' Dad said. 'Get the phone.'

Sam made one of his noises, but he stood up to answer it.

'Hello?' He paused. Then he slammed the receiver. 'Fuck.'

Dad and I looked at him. 'What?'

'That was Mum.'

I jumped up off the bench, and the phone started ringing again.

'Leave it,' Sam said.

I looked at Dad, but he said nothing. He was the only one still sitting down.

The phone kept ringing.

'Iris,' my brother warned.

I looked at him.

Silverweed

'If you pick up that phone ...' He didn't finish his sentence, which was much scarier than if he did.

I couldn't help it, though. 'Sorry,' I said. And I picked it up. 'Hello?'

'Iris?'

The kitchen grew enormous around me. She sounded so far away and quiet that I thought she must be in another country.

'Is that you?'

'Mmhmm.'

'Oh Iris, it's so lovely to ...' her sentence stopped, and I could tell she was crying.

I ran my index finger down the inside of numbers three, six and nine, collecting a line of sticky dust. I wanted to tell her it was OK, and ask where she was, to stretch the phone cord into the living room and shut the door, and settle into Dad's green armchair, but I could feel Sam listening, and Dad sitting down just behind me, so I stayed where I was.

'You still there?'

'Yeah.'

'I've missed you so much. I'm so sorry I've not ...'

I ran my finger between the next column of numbers, rubbing the black sticky dust into a ball.

'Are you OK?'

'Yeah.'

'You're very quiet.'

I picked at a piece of dry skin on my lip.

'I've missed you. How are you? What've you been doing? Is your brother OK?'

'Mmhmm.'

'Was that your dad that answered before?'

Without thinking, I lied. 'Yeah.'

'And you're both all right?'

'Mmhmm.'

'And your Dad? He's ... coping?'

I started cleaning between the one, four, seven.

'Sorry Iris, I ... How are you? Tell me something.'

I tried to think.

'Anything.'

Chelsey Flood

'Erm ...'

'It doesn't matter what.'

'I'm ... I'm just having my tea ...'

'Oh.' She paused. 'OK. Sorry sweetheart. You should have said. I'll let you go then. Just a minute ... Can I ring again? Same time next week?'

The kitchen was so quiet.

'Iris?'

'I don't know.'

She inhaled, and I thought of her on her own somewhere, in a phone box.

'OK.'

There was no sound for a few seconds and I wondered if she had gone, but then she spoke and her voice sounded different. 'Oh! It's so lovely to speak to you, I'm so glad you're OK! Give my love to Sam, won't you? Tell him I love him. I love you both. Now, go and eat your tea and I'll give you a call, next week, same time, OK?'

'OK.'

'I can't wait.'

'No.'

'I love you.'

'OK.'

'And I'll see you soon.'

'Yeah. OK then. Bye.'

The kitchen shrank as I replaced the receiver, and I stood there, waiting for somebody to say something.

Chelsey Flood has had short stories published in *The Big Issue*, *Riptide* and Route's *Born in the 1980s* anthology. She is currently being mentored by Bernardine Evaristo as part of the 2010 Jerwood/Arvon mentoring scheme. *Silverweed* is the story of Iris Dancy and how her life changes the summer that the gypsies come.

Tim Harding

Balloon Rangers

Cuticles

Balloon Rangers

Egbert fell from a great height and landed uninjured. He stayed curled up in a ball for about a minute before chancing his arm and slowly straightening out. He stood for another minute and then opened one of his eyes. He was standing on a small white planetoid. The surface of this earth was translucent. Bringing his eye close to the ground he could see the interior. It was as featureless within as without.

'Cor,' said Egbert. He opened his other eye. A woodlouse was watching him. The woodlouse gave him a curt little nod.

'Hello,' said Egbert. 'How's it going?'

'Could be worse, mate. Could be worse. You all right?'

'Yeah. I thought I was a goner after I fell from a great height, but it looks like everything's in one piece.' He flexed his rows of legs to make sure. Everything was fine.

'No surprises there,' said the woodlouse. 'You're a woodlouse, mate. We get along all right.'

'True enough,' said Egbert.

The other woodlouse, having discharged his duty, turned around and started walking away. Egbert watched him go. The planet wasn't big enough to go very far, though, and the woodlouse had to stop before the curve got too steep and he fell off. Egbert, lacking anything else to do, pulled up alongside him. The woodlouse was peering down into the darkness of space.

'Nice night, isn't it?' said Egbert. No reply.
'My name's Egbert.'
'You're a chatty sort, aren'tcha?'
'I like talking to people.'
The woodlouse chuckled bleakly. 'I didn't think I qualified,' he muttered.
'Us isopods have to stick together,' said Egbert.
'You've got the common touch all right, mate,' then, after a little consideration, 'I'm Cedric.'
'Pleased to meet you,' said Egbert, shuffling his segments in greeting.
'Pleased to meet,' echoed Cedric, and gave another little nod, waggling his feelers a bit.
'How long have you been here?' asked Egbert, patting the springy ground with one of his feet.
Cedric sighed. 'Somewhere between long enough and not long enough,' he said.
Egbert felt like he was missing an implication. Sometimes it's just impossible to understand other people, he thought to himself.
'I suppose you fell from that there tree,' said Cedric, pointing a feeler up to the apple tree that formed a canopy overhead.
'Yeah,' chuckled Egbert. 'It was a bit of a nightmare.'
'What happened?' asked Cedric. He seemed interested.
'It was a bird, man.'
'Oh shit!' Cedric cackled.
'Yeah!' said Egbert. 'The cunt landed on the branch like *that* far away from me.' Egbert indicated a distance with his feelers.
'Oh God!' moaned Cedric.
'So it hasn't seen me, and I'm just there thinking, "don't do anything, don't even move".'
'You've got to keep yer 'ead down, son. It's the best thing you can do for yourself.'
'And the bloody thing hasn't even seen me, but suddenly it's hopping down the branch in my direction tweeting like a banshee. I curl up in a ball – '
'Good move, mate.'
' – I curl up in a ball and the bloody thing just boots me with its foot,

and I fall to my certain death! The worst part is it never even knew I was there.'

'Quite a story,' said Cedric, shaking his head. 'You had a lucky escape there, I don't mind telling you.'

'I know, man. I know.'

Cedric resumed gazing into the abyss. 'Makes you think, doesn't it?' he said quietly.

'How long have you been on this planet?' asked Egbert, tapping the floor with his foot again.

'This?' Cedric mimicked the movement. 'S'not a planet. It's a balloon. Like for parties an' that.'

'Oh right,' said Egbert, not really understanding. 'I've been out of the loop for a while.'

'Yeah. Well. I dunno,' said Cedric. 'Not like any of us have really got a backstage pass or nothing.'

'I suppose not,' said Egbert. 'But then again, I used to be a butterfly, and before that I was a cat, but when I was a butterfly I didn't remember being a cat. Now that I'm a woodlouse, I remember being a butterfly and a cat and a bunch of other things as well.'

'How was it being a cat?' asked Cedric. 'Good?'

'It was stressful,' said Egbert.

'I could see that being the case.'

'I think I prefer being a woodlouse. I'm surprised they let us remember about *reincarnation* and all that, though. I thought if they let anyone know it would be the scarabs or something.'

'Nope,' said Cedric in a flat voice. 'Only woodlice. "The favoured sons." Hmph. I've talked to some scarab beetles in my time. They might know something about something, but they don't know nothing about this. The reincarnation or what-have-you.'

'Made me want to kick myself when I found out, though,' said Egbert, shrugging his carapace in an expression of embarrassment. 'I was a man, way back when, then I die and they ask me what I want to come back as. Now I had never really thought about it before but then I decide a cat is a good idea, because I reckon it's got a nice peaceful life. Just eats and has sex and lies around in the sun.'

Cedric scoffed.

Tim Harding

'Yeah, I know. I should have listened to the guy. There he was, all going, "All beings so far have created something beyond themselves; do you want to be the ebb of this great flood, and even go back to the beasts rather than overcome man?" And I'm just thinking *I can't wait to be a cat. It's going to be great.* So anyway, I come back as a cat and instantly forget ever being a man. Then it turns out being a cat feels pretty stressful when you're a cat. Walking around all the time. Catching things. Not getting run over. Who needs it? So then when it comes to the time again, I ask for a peaceful life as a butterfly and so on and so on. I mean, it's fine, but I can't help thinking it's a bit of a downward spiral. Mind you, I suppose it happens to the best of us. Lots of woodlice probably in the same boat as me.'

'Hmph,' said Cedric. 'Wouldn't catch me doing that. Mug's game.'

'But you must have been something before you were a woodlouse,' said Egbert.

'Woodlouse,' said Cedric. 'Just woodlouse, over and over again.'

'Didn't they give you a choice?' said Egbert.

'Yeah. They've made me choose a lot of times,' said Cedric. 'And I choose woodlouse. Keep yer 'ead down, that's my philosophy. Don't upset the cart. Nothing wrong with woodlouse.'

Egbert looked at Cedric's blank face.

'You never wanted to try out being a man?' Egbert asked. 'Or something even better?'

'Nah,' said Cedric. 'No point to it. Besides, you were a man, and you just came straight back to woodlouse in no time flat.'

'That's a fair point,' said Egbert. He looked down into the night and thought about being a man. 'It was quite exciting sometimes,' he said.

'Nah,' said Cedric, 'Listen. You've made your way from man to woodlouse, and much in you is still man. Me, I've been walking this woodlouse path since before man were invented. I'm a woodlouse through and through. I recognise a good thing when I've got it.' Cedric stared steadily straight forward, at nothing in particular.

'Well,' said Egbert, 'it's your life.'

'That it is,' said Cedric.

Egbert thought he could see the sky beginning to pale through the gaps in the canopy.

'Well I'm off, then,' said Egbert. 'Nice talking to you, man. What did you say your name was again?'
'Cedric.'
'Nice talking to you, Cedric. See you around.'
'Bye.'
Egbert shuffled down the slope of the balloon and looked to the ground. He thought he could see grass or stone or something, but wasn't sure quite what. Lifting his feet and curling into a ball, he fell into the darkness.

CUTICLES

'Strap on these yeti goggles,' he growled, 'and let's go!'
Nothing happened.
Yeti Goggles has been cancelled. We have not the requisite skill.

I reached out very slowly; pressed hairy tendrils into concrete pores; spread green fans, absorbed light and grew some more. I was ivy.

Someone jizzed in a plastic cup. Later on, Stifler drank it. (At least that's how I remember it.)

We had assumed they wouldn't like us drinking Carling on the field behind the chemistry block.
    'Morning, boys,' said Dr Ryan on his way to the staffroom. He looked sad.

Sharon didn't wake up the next morning. Just lay beside me without life.

No one knew why the prosecutor stood that close to the fire. It couldn't have been comfortable, but he sure cut a dashing silhouette. When Sharon's fat spat, and got in his face, no one saw him lick his moustache.

So what if Jesus was skeletal and intimidating, with skin and clothes the colour of oxidised copper? So what if His palms and shoulders bristled with dirty steel spines, and He leaned at an unnatural angle? He is still our Lord.

I'd started getting an unusual amount of condensation on my window. Water soaked through the tea towel on the windowsill and then pooled on the floor, making a mush of the receipts and class handouts that I had left there. Black mould started bustling up from the skirting board and then framed the entire window. Mustardy yellow stalactites descended, forming bars. The glass itself disappeared beneath a creamy fungus the colour of mandarin sorbet. That was the beginning, then came the middle, and now here's the end.

After I started exploring the abandoned cinema, I found that each screen was a portal into a different unformed world. I had to start playing movies there again so that the little worlds could grow to maturity by copying things from the films. Honestly, it was great. I used to play that one about a talking hovercraft on every screen, so that each world I visited could be explored in a sassy talking hovercraft. I made a Western World, a Romcom World. All that kind of stuff. I didn't make a Horror World because no one wants to live in a Horror World. Think about it. It

would be terrifying. My mum said that I was playing God but that she didn't mind.

A star was born. Gases burned incredibly for several hundred million years before dispersing. There was not much in the way of organic life orbiting it. It wasn't one of those stars.

To rescue a beautiful princess, I had to engage in mortal combat with a horrible ogre, and that fight never stops.

Mohammed grabbed Sadhia's collar and hurled her headfirst into the cobweb. The lattice of sticky, invisible silk on her face had been secreted from the spider's abdomen. This all happened a few years ago now.

One day they just fucking pushed me too far, goddamnit. That day I just went home and read all the books. The next morning, someone asked me if I had read *Powerful Gemstones* by Adam England. 'Yes,' I replied without hesitation, and a corona of hot light scorched the fucker from the face of the earth. 'I have read all the books!' I bellowed, and the light destroyed the entire university. Nobody called Norwich a fine city after that.

'Tweezers,' said Professor Westerby. My hand was trembling, and the tweezers rang like a tuning fork until he closed his rubber glove around them. The stillness of the man spread through my arm when we touched. A gentle paralysis held me. 'Let go of it,' said Professor Westerby. I looked up, and let go. Seconds later, a slimy red bullet rattled in a pan. 'The hardest part is over now,' he said.

He was wrong, though. The hardest part came months later, when the seagull's chicks no longer recognised their mother.

Tim Harding has studied English and Creative Writing at the Universities of Sussex, Kent and East Anglia. He is currently writing his second novel, about sexy apocalyptic adventures on the back of a giant monster. He'd love to hear from you.

Alex Ivey

Kingdoms

From Kingdoms, *a young adult fantasy novel in which troubled teenager Sarah, meets Annie, a cantankerous elderly woman with a terrible secret to tell. Eventually, Sarah must confront her own problems in order to finish what Annie started in 1930s Vermont. This excerpt is taken from the beginning of Annie's story.*

After lunch the next day, Annie sat on her back porch waiting for Tom. She had her shoes next to her – it was just too hot to put them on. Next to them was the bag she'd filled with the stolen goods for the fort: the spare sheet from her parents' room, a couple of pillows to sit on, and a garden trowel. She sat on the top step, letting her legs hang over the edge as she traced a circle with her finger on the decking. Round and round, round and round.

'You ready?'

She looked up and saw Tom standing in front of her, grinning.

'What're you so happy about?'

He pointed to the bag slung over his shoulder. 'My ma baked brownies yesterday.'

Annie smiled and started putting on her shoes. 'Did you manage to get anything else?'

'Yeah. A blanket – thought maybe we could use it for the roof.'

'Good. Let's go.'

The grass behind the house spread out into a pachysandra patch which crawled out low over the ground and led into the woods. As they

marched among the leathery green leaves, the trees suddenly thickened and their ivy-wrapped trunks twisted together, so Annie and Tom had to push past the brambles and thickets to get inside. Once they were in, though, it opened for them into a great expanse with sloping, worn paths snaking this way and that, the afternoon light carefully picking which trees, which flowers to rest on. The ground was a marriage of greens, as the ferns, moss and grass mixed and wound through each other, then broke with surges of purple, yellow and pink as wildflowers forced their way through in confident bursts.

'Follow me.' Annie walked past Tom, along the stream, taking him deeper into the forest, birches gleaming white on either side of them, the paths between the trees becoming less and less worn until they disappeared completely. The distant sounds of birds calling to each other were the only reminder of life outside the forest. As they walked on, the ground began to slope upwards, gradually becoming steeper and steeper, and making them stop to catch their breath. Then it suddenly leveled off at a small clearing, and at the center was a giant hemlock that dominated all the other trees around it.

'Here,' said Annie.

They walked up to the clearing, and as they got closer, Annie reached out and carefully pushed aside the heavy boughs that fanned the ground. She tucked her head down slightly as she went inside, leaving Tom standing outside alone.

'C'mon!' Annie stuck her hand through the branches and gestured for him to follow.

Tom quickly did as Annie had done. Inside, the space was just tall enough for the two of them to stand up on the soft earth floor. The boughs enveloped the area so completely that only tiny amounts of light could seep in between the hemlock's needles, giving the inside a dark, subtle glow. Tom's mouth fell open as he looked around. Annie watched him.

'This is great!' he said. 'D'you come here a lot?'

Every chance I get. She shrugged. 'Once in a while.'

Tom reached up and grasped a thick branch just above their heads that cut across the space inside the hemlock. 'We can use this to make the roof.' He jerked his head sharply to the right. 'Hey! What's that?'

Annie looked where he was pointing, but whatever he'd seen was gone too quickly. 'What was it?'

'I don't know,' said Tom. 'Must've been a bird or somethin'. But it looked like *eyes!*' He laughed.

'You're strange.' Annie giggled.

He smiled and nodded towards Annie's bag. 'You got a sheet in there?'

She pulled out her parents' sheet and handed it to Tom.

'Hmmm ...' he said. 'This is kinda small.' He wadded it up and put it to one side. 'Let's use my blanket – it might be too heavy, but we can try and see.' He took it out and bunched it up into a long, sloppy roll and hung it over the branch, then grabbed one side and tugged it along, then dragged the other side to center it. 'Now you take one end, and I'll take the other. Then we have to find somethin' to hold it up at both ends.'

Annie did as she was told. She scanned the area but couldn't find anything to prop up the blanket on her side. She looked back at Tom, who had already pulled his end through the branches and out to the other side.

'I think this'll hold for now,' he said. 'What are you gonna use?'

Her end wouldn't reach all the way through, so she had to find something else.

'Break off a branch an' stick it in the ground. You know, like in a teepee.' He reached out for Annie's half. 'Give it here. I'll hold it while you get the stick.'

Annie walked over to the tree and eventually found a spray thin enough for her to break off, but hopefully sturdy enough to hold up the blanket without bending. She pulled as hard as she could, but couldn't get it off.

'Step on it, hard! Kick it!' Tom shouted.

Annie stamped, but it wouldn't budge.

'Harder!'

Annie bristled. She stopped for a moment to catch her breath and heard a rustling to her left. As she turned to see what it was, she heard a loud crack and looked back at the branch. It had started to come away from the tree.

'Kick it again!' Tom called from the other side.

Alex Ivey

Annie's face contorted into a scowl, and she kicked as hard as she could, her foot colliding with the sprig and sending it flying forwards. She stumbled, then quickly recovered herself, picked up the branch and walked back to Tom. She dug a small hole with the trowel and widened it with her foot. She held the stick vertically over her head for a moment, and then rammed it down into the ground with all the force she could muster. She let it go. It stayed.

'There,' she said.

Tom handed her the blanket, pulled it over the branch, and stood back to see what they'd made. Annie smiled. It already looked like a fort.

'Not bad, huh? I'll go look around for some good rocks we can use for seats and things,' Tom said and went out into the woods.

Annie decided that the far corner of her half would be the potion-making area and made a mental note to take one of her mother's mixing bowls that night after she'd gone to sleep. In the meantime, she'd dig a hole where the bowl would go. It would be like a cauldron, but in the ground. Kneeling down, she dragged her bag over and took out the trowel. As she dug, she wondered if Tom had ever made a potion before. She'd have to show him where to get the berries that gave the best color and the plants that had the gooiest insides when you tore open their stalks. But they'd have to watch out for poison ivy – did they even have that down South? It didn't matter; she'd tell him what to watch out for.

Annie looked down at the hole and realized that she'd already dug too deep – the mixing bowl would be far too small for it now. She'd just have to get a bigger bowl. Or a bucket. And they'd just have to make more potion. So she kept digging. And digging. She dug so hard that the wooden handle on the trowel snapped off and splintered into her hand. She managed to pull out the biggest pieces from her palm but left the smaller ones to deal with later. The soil felt so cool and fresh as she pressed her hands into it that she couldn't feel the splinters' sting anymore – she could get more done with both hands anyway. So she kept digging. She pushed her hands in the soft, dark earth and tightened them into fists, clumping the dirt in tight balls before throwing them to one side onto a growing pile which was alive with armadillo bugs and centipedes. She could feel the ants crawling over her hands and the worms slipping over and around her fingers. The smell was intoxicating:

the deeper she got, the cleaner and richer it smelled. The hole was now so deep that she had to get inside it to keep working.

'Sorry I took so long – hey, didn't anyone ever tell you you'd get to China if you dug deep enough? You're gonna fall out the other side!' Tom laughed.

Annie turned around and gazed up at Tom but didn't really see him. She studied her hands and saw they were almost black with dirt, the underside of her fingernails so full of earth that it had started to push back into her nail beds. She kept digging.

'Found these big stones out there by the stream. We can use 'em as seats, or maybe even this big flat one as a table. What d'you think?'

No answer.

'You want one of them brownies?'

Nothing.

'What're you doing anyway? You buryin' something?'

Again, nothing.

'Annie? Annie! Hello?!?'

Annie just dug and dug and dug.

'I'm gonna have to get going soon, Annie – hey! What's that?'

Something glinted in the dirt. But Annie had felt it before she'd seen it. Knew there was something there. Something for her. She scratched at the earth where the flash was, ran her fingers around its edges and dug, creating a neat oval around the spot. Once the trough was deep enough, she sank her fingers in as far as she could. Something cold and hard. As soon as she touched it, she felt a shiver run through her from top to bottom. She pulled it out of the earth.

'What is it?'

With her back to Tom, Annie sat on her heels and leaned over the treasure in her hands. Despite the sticky heat of the day, she was suddenly very, very cold. Like steel. And just as strong.

'Can I see it?'

And just as she'd felt before she'd dug it out, she knew it was hers. Like it had been made for her and no one else.

'Annie?'

She closed her eyes and held it tightly in her hand, the icy cold racing through her as if it had been injected directly into her veins.

Alex Ivey

'Annie, lemme see it.'

Annie looked up. 'Oh, I ... it's ...' Her eyes fell back down to her hands.

'C'mon, it's not like it's yours.'

'You said you had to go home, Tom.'

'I just want to look at it!'

'It's time to go, Tom.'

'OK, OK! God.'

Silence.

'What happened to the trowel?'

'Oh, yeah,' Annie glanced over at the broken remains as she wrapped her prize in one of the towels before placing it back in her bag. 'I broke it.'

'You *broke* it? How'd you do *that*?'

'Don't know. It just happened.'

'Jeez, Annie,' Tom said, his eyes wide.

Annie looked around the fort. 'Ready?'

'Uh, yeah.' He stuffed the now dried-out brownies in the bag and threw it over his shoulder. 'Let's go.'

They parted the tree's boughs and walked together out of the fort and into the woods. Annie smiled to herself as she went.

Alex Ivey studied English Literature at Boston University and moved to the UK in 1999. Before starting the MA at UEA, she worked in the voluntary sector managing services for older people. She is originally from Connecticut.

Richard Lambert

Magic Earth
A Novel

Chapter One

The fog lay heavy. Thick banks had rolled in, slipping through chain-link fences and crossing building sites and rail lines, groping down passages, settling over wasteground, hanging above canals and getting caught in the fingers of trees. It hovered at the entrances to tunnels and erased blocks of flats and soaked washing on their balconies, and it drowned the blinking red lights of towers in the City and on the Isle of Dogs. It billowed in successive waves, huddled on spongy school playgrounds, looked in at the windows of libraries, and glossed the roofs of cars and leaves of suburban gardens with bubbles of dew, and dampened the clothes and skins of anyone fool enough to be out in it. People shivered and saw no further than a dozen yards and wondered at what had been conjured from such ordinary objects as parking meters and telephone boxes, where the world seemed altered by a dream.

Towards midnight everything grew still and in fact it seemed for moments at a time that the entire capital had gone to sleep and as if those shocks and raptures that London daily, nightly, courted, had never been, or were a temporary existence, and only the fog was real. And then, past one o'clock, the rumbling underground system stopped, the fog grew thicker, and towards one particular suburb, on a bridge above the north circular, and beneath the nimbus of a streetlight, all that could be heard was the moisture trickling along the roadside. And then past two o'clock, even that ceased.

For a moment, on that bridge, there was a complete silence and stillness. Then a spot in the fog lightened. It brightened and continued to intensify in brightness until suddenly, spray-kissed, its blue light sprawling across the fog like a lighthouse beam, an ambulance roared out of the fog. It sped upwards of fifty miles an hour, headlamps wide.

Alone in the cab, tiny Miranda gripped the wheel, scanning the vapour and wanting to bat it away as it clutched for the windscreen. She crossed the bridge, passed some allotments, then slowed to a crawl through traffic lights, revved the vehicle up a hill, then began the long scoot down towards St John's Wood, the fog thinning and Miranda breathing more easily, gunning the engine on the straights, humming Beyoncé and hoping Control would find her a hospital before the overdose of tricyclics mixed with vodka killed the woman in the back.

Her partner came through the dividing door.

'She doesn't look well.' He seated himself and took the mike. 'Control, this is F31, any idea where we're going?'

Shops dwindled, white-out bloomed. Timbers loomed, strung with black nets: a zoo. In the seal enclosure, grey seals honked under the September trees, sending after the ambulance sad songs as it vanished on its voyage.

In the cab, the radio voice spoke. 'Roger, F31. We've got you either the Royal London or Bart's. Awaiting confirmation.'

'Roger, Control. Priority call. Acute overdose. TCAs with alcohol. Hypotension, cardiac dysrhythmia. Potential MI.'

'Roger. Thanks for your patience.'

Miranda stared through the windscreen at the whiteness rushing for them.

'Nice out,' her partner said, hung the mike handset in its cradle, and scrambled back through the door.

On Gower Street the fog grew dense. Miranda slowed. She sang Beyoncé now and considered their passengers: the dying woman and the woman's teenage son, Patrick, who had found his mother at shortly after one. Miranda and her partner had reached them after an RTA job at about one forty to find the woman screaming she was going to have a heart attack, and in fact, she might yet arrest. The woman had begun hallucinating but couldn't tell them when she'd taken the pills. The son

Patrick had ummed and ahed: midnight maybe, maybe earlier. Miranda had thought: probably watching *Wife Swap* or *Question Time*. That'd just about do it. But in terms of timescale, a mid- to late-evening OD gave them around ... no time at all. And with Hendon and the Royal Free at capacity, it meant this yomp into the centre while Control found them space. But they needed to be where they were going. Like, now.

But time slipped by as if it was fog, and the fog itself thickened. Miranda made the turn at the bottom of Gower Street and would not have been surprised to see a whale moving down High Holborn towards her, the mist was that thick. Her foot hung above the brake.

'F31,' the radio voice said. 'This is Control. We can confirm Resuss at St Bartholomew's. Confirm St Bartholomew's. Blueing you in.'

Miranda glanced across and debated between shouting for her partner to acknowledge or reaching for the mike herself. Finally, she leaned a long way over and, as she did so, the fog parted to reveal a figure standing in the middle of the road.

Miranda kicked the brake and swore. Her body was flung forward and restrained by the seat belt. Tyres shrieked, equipment banged, and her partner called out. She felt the rear of the ambulance slide around from behind her. She lifted the brake pedal, jabbed downwards two, three, four times, thought of death.

The ambulance continued to skid.

Slowed; stopped.

Silence. Fog.

The figure stood before her not two yards away.

For a moment she thought it was an angel. For another moment Miranda stared at the semi-naked young man. He wore long silver boots, tight silver shorts, a short silver cape, a silver eye-mask; he was otherwise naked. His hands rested on his hips, and he swayed. Adrenalin sped through Miranda and she shouted, hoarsely, 'You stupid fuck!' He swayed. 'Get out my fucking way!'

'F31, can confirm Resuss at St Bartholomew's. Acknowledge please.'

Miranda punched the button for the siren. The man rocked but didn't move away. Setting the siren to a histrionic trill, she swung the steering wheel, power-assisted but still a mighty twist and was glad, no, proud of her three-times-a-week weight-training sessions as she took herself and

the three in the back – her partner, the dying woman and her red-haired son Patrick – around the derelict figure. She looked out as she went around – the guy's eyes were unfocused and he had silver glitter in his hair – and lowering the window to cold London air, she said, 'You stupid. Fucking. Arsehole,' then raised the window, reached for the mike, acknowledged Bart's, and drove the last few hundred yards. She rolled in under the arch to the silent courtyard of trees and dark pavilions and parked cars. It was 2.27am.

Red-haired Patrick stepped down into the courtyard. He had to let go his mum's hand and watched her, strapped on a trolley under a red blanket, being wheeled up a ramp and into the hospital. He rubbed his head where he'd hit it when the ambulance had skidded. The weird shapes of what looked like beach huts and cedar of Lebanon trees bulked from the fog. It was too much. His head throbbed strongly. He hurried after his mum.

As he entered the resuscitation room, someone shouted, 'She's arrested!' and his mum was unclipped, undressed and her sad, pale flesh was lifted onto the bed. Her chest was spattered with jelly, pads were placed, someone shouted, and his mum jumped vertically. A nurse worked a tube down her throat and he caught his breath because she was waving her arms like she was drowning, but then the medics were less frantic and drip bags were hung on a thin metal tree, and the tiny paramedic from the ambulance spoke to a doctor. Her lips were purple now, his mum's, and her arms cotton-wool rubbed and plunged with catheters. Then the medics seemed to step away and the electrocardiogram began its horrible boring work and the ventilator pressed and gasped like a deep-sea diver's aqualung.

'Hello, I'm Dr Aziz?' said a doctor, approaching. 'Patrick?'

He glanced at her.

'Patrick? I understand your mum's taken a mix of alcohol and her medication? Can you tell me what happened?'

He opened his mouth to speak. 'Is she ...?'

'We're doing all we can to help her? To do that, we need to know what she took and when? Do you know what time she took her medication?'

Patrick looked to the doctor. She kept her eyes on his and after a few moments, he noticed his breathing, shallow, barely there, and took a deep breath. He blew out hard.

'Patrick?'

'I was asleep.'

'And what time did you wake up?'

'Something woke me up.'

'Yes?'

'I knew I had to go downstairs.'

'Yes?'

'She said she was going to die and she was making noises like she was, you know, like there was something caught in her throat. She didn't try to kill herself, she didn't mean that.' Patrick closed his eyes. Opened them. 'Is she going to … ?' He couldn't finish.

'We're going to help her?' It was difficult to tell when she was asking a question. It was all question. 'What time was this?'

'Er … One o'clock.'

'Do you know how many she took?'

That was his job, to know things like that. He frowned hard, looked down. He had messed up again.

'Is she taking any other medication?'

'No.'

'No she's not?'

Patrick raised his eyes. The doctor's eyes were brown and pretty. Slowly, he nodded.

'You're sure?'

Patrick nodded. He was sure: someone had to be.

'Is she a regular drug user?'

He shook his head.

'Does she drink heavily?'

'No.' He stroked the back of his neck.

'It's important?'

'A bit. Nothing, you know.' He blushed, frowned, clenched his teeth, stroked his neck furiously. She wasn't meant to drink anything on the antidepressants. His eyes got hot. 'Sorry.'

Dr Aziz smiled kindly. 'We need to do our work now, we have a

relatives' room here?'

Patrick wanted to ask if his mum was going to be all right. But he couldn't. 'What are you going to do to her?'

'We'll give her charcoal and – '

There was a great sound from the bed, like the beating of a swan's wings or laundered sheets flapped out on the wind. His mother had half sat up. Her eyes were wild and she began dragging the tube out of her throat. Dr Aziz ran over. And then, from behind him, someone gripped Patrick's upper arm strongly and a nurse walked him out of the resuscitation room like he was somewhere he wasn't meant to be at all.

Richard Lambert is from Bristol, has a PhD in medieval history, and is writing a novel, *Magic Earth*, about a teenage boy's journey across Britain. *The Rialto* published a pamphlet of his poetry in 2008.

Ben Lyle

Terms
A Novel

I can't be expected to remember everything.

You people always need the details. Exact times, places, dates. As if I'd been taking notes, watching Mervyn's every move. Life isn't like that, at least not for a man like me. Maybe if I'd been one of those diary-keeping girls, with swirly writing and circles above the 'i's, with big fat hearts and exclamation marks. But is it even like that for those girls? That's a make-believe world too. They find that out the first time Clive or Jake or John or whoever waltzes off with someone else and cleaves their big fat heart in twain.

What I will say is that Mervyn was the best teacher I ever had, bar none. It's as well to understand that, if you understand nothing else.

*

Autumn 1986

My best friend Charlie and I sat in the school library on the Sunday before the first day of term. As boarders, we arrived at the weekend to settle in and soon found ourselves alone at work. We shared a large wooden table, its edges striped by penknives. Charlie had been tutored in science over the holidays and took me through some basic physics. As he scrabbled around for his calculator, I turned to the window and gazed out over the gravel, past the sloping football pitch towards the meadow. Grey, green, greener and then again grey – the low dark grey of the troubled Scottish sky.

At that moment a fast-moving figure stalked across the gravel, his face determined and serious. The library took up a corner of the Main House, so I watched him as he marched around our flank with swift, precise strides. He had wild shoulder-length hair. His beard reached from his nose to the top of his chest and stretched from ear-to-ear unchecked. Amid the inky bushes of his face lay two ale-dark eyes and a swollen red nose. He looked like an escapee from The Muppets.

'It's the yeti!' Charlie giggled, scrambling to the next window. 'Who is he?' he said as the stranger strode off.

'That's Mervyn, the new Math teacher,' a voice answered in a sharp Canadian accent. Fran, the part-time cook and sometime history teacher stood behind us. The teachers often doubled up jobs, Bannock House was that kind of school, everything a bit vague around the edges. 'What are you two boys doing in here?'

'Nothing,' I said just as Charlie blurted out, 'Physics.' He tugged at one of his ginger curls. 'My physics homework. From home.'

'Physics!' Fran barked. She pushed chairs against the walls, loudly clearing a space on the floor. 'You're only twelve. You kids should be running around or something.'

'There's nothing wrong with science,' I said, feeling bad for Charlie. He always trusted people with his thoughts.

Fran dipped her chin and looked at me through round, rimless glasses. 'Not now, James.'

'If this was a proper school,' I went on. 'You'd be –'

'I heard it before, remember? Listen, scram. It's the staff meditation session in here.'

I opened my mouth but Charlie touched me on the arm. 'Let's go,' he said. 'We can finish this later.'

As we skipped down the wonky front steps of the Main House, Charlie pointed in the direction Mervyn had gone. 'You know, I think that new teacher was wearing a tie. Did you see it?' he said in excitement. A tie was not typical wear for the staff at the school. On that afternoon, for example, Fran wore clogs, flared orange trousers and a fringed poncho.

'I'm not sure,' I said.

'Let's take a look,' Charlie said. 'I'll race you.'

I pulled ahead, laughing, as we chased after Mervyn. It felt good to

run with someone again. I'd spent the summer holidays pretty much on my own, which was nothing new, and had forgotten what it was like to run wherever you wanted, to take off without worrying about the traffic, or strangers or coming home to an empty house. Charlie made it all seem normal and not stupid or childish or anything. It didn't really matter to me where we were going, I sprinted ahead, listening to Charlie's panting as he tried to keep up.

'Ooomph!' he cried. I turned to see him stretched out, face in the stone-studded path, arms splayed. 'I tripped.' He held up a scuffed palm, flecked red.

'Dipstick,' I said. 'I told you to get a belt.' I hauled him up by his elbow. A sunbeam burst through the heavy clouds, dappling his face for a second.

'It wasn't my trousers.' He pretended to be angry. 'Know-it-all.' I looked back towards the Main House. I didn't know when it had been built but it felt too old. It was made from dirty, unbrushed stones of different sizes with only a window here and there. It swallowed the sun. Round about it, trees bubbled like gigantic broccoli. The building looked like an overgrown gravestone in mourning for itself.

I saw Fran moving around in the library before she reached up and shut the curtains, banning the light. 'We've lost him now,' I said.

'Let's cut through the Tangle.' Charlie hiked up his loose jeans. 'If he's going to Dungowan we'll see him on the road,' he went on, ever hopeful. The clouds shuttered, sending a shadow racing back towards the house. I glanced at Charlie. I'd almost forgotten what it was like to have someone smiling full in your face, as if it were you that made them happy.

We struck off the path. The Tangle was an area of the school grounds that no one really bothered with. A huge triangle of overgrown land off the track that led to the lodge and the southern exit, it stretched to the river on one side and the road to the nearest village on the other. I'd only ever been in there once, in my first term, but never explored it properly. A couple of times Charlie suggested we take a look but I'd never seen the point before.

Trees, bushes and long grass grew together like a complex sci-fi monster. When you pulled one branch out of your face, something else

twanged yards away. The ground was wet underfoot, the kind of damp that made you feel that it could never be dry, even if the sun shone for a hundred years. Every footstep squelched and slid. Charlie chattered on about his holiday, about his irritating little sister and the granny with one eye and too many hairs on her upper lip. I liked hearing about his family.

It was hard work slashing through the Tangle and we quickly realised Mervyn would be long gone, even if he had been going to the village. In the rush I'd forgotten that we'd see him soon enough, anyway. He was a teacher, not a visitor. We decided to try to get to the road all the same, to see if we could do it. I crawled under a low cross branch, urging Charlie to follow. In the distance we heard cars arriving at the Main House, girls screaming their reunions. It wouldn't be much fun back there. I could never think of the right thing to say, at least not without Charlie to translate.

When I first arrived, the year before, that moment on the front gravel was the worst. Left there, on your own, watching everybody else's excitement. Kids threaded between knots of adults, shouting and laughing. Parents by their cars, holding coats and bags in arms like branches. Even the newer children seemed to know each other, somehow. My mother said she had to get the five-fifteen and left, using the same cab in which we'd come.

'You must be James.' Fran bustled over to me, though I didn't know her name then. 'Where's your mom?'

'She had to catch the train back to London,' I said. 'We're busy people.'

'Right,' she said, confused. She offered her ringless hand. 'I'm Fran.'

A stray drop of rain splashed onto my too-new raincoat. I flicked up the hood and looked down. Fran shouted to someone over my head and wandered away.

'Hello,' said the owner of a pair of white Nike trainers with the red tick. 'I'm Charlie.' I looked up into his face, grateful he was the same height as me. 'I think we're sharing a room. Come on, it's this way.'

I followed him across the gravel as he pushed through a thicket of twittering girls towards a side door of the Main House. Charlie called to

a few of them as we passed and I heard a couple sing out to him good-naturedly and laugh.

'We're on the middle-landing,' he went on as we shuffled along a gloomy corridor. Dull light spilled in through half-opened doors and Charlie's voice echoed into the unseen depths of the house. 'Our room's pretty big. Bigger than the others, anyway.' We climbed steel-capped stairs and crossed a large square landing with five doors off it. My feet stuck to the black and white chessboard lino. 'You can have whichever bed you want, I don't mind. I hope you don't snore. Where are you from? Do you grind your teeth?'

'What?' I said, bringing my hand up to my jaw, worried that it showed somehow.

'Oh good, you speak,' he threw my bag on a single bed by the window. 'So you grind your teeth? I'm only asking because my dad's a dentist. Look, don't be shy – if you do, it's cool. We're sharing, so you may as well tell me.'

'How long have you been here?' I asked.

'About an hour,' he said looking at his watch.

'An hour? But I thought …'

'Everyone's really friendly here,' he said, struggling with the sash window. 'Considering it's my first day at the school. God, this thing's really stuck.'

I stepped over, flipped the catch and levered the sash up in one swift movement.

'Oh great.' He smiled with a mouth full of braces, like a good dentist's son. 'We're a team.'

Those words came back to me as we fought through the Tangle in our failed effort to follow Mervyn. 'We're a team.' Scrambling under a briar, I came across a small, cobbled-together wooden hut. The older kids made them from cheap timber the school used for fuel. Huts were all over the grounds, mostly in trees, private places for cigarettes, beer and snogging. I'd only ever been in one before. When Charlie had an invite once on Midsummer's Eve, he took me with him. I didn't expect to find one in the Tangle, though. It seemed like too much hassle. 'Charlie,' I shouted. 'Over here!'

Ben Lyle

From the outside the hut looked ramshackle and abandoned. About four feet high, it sat on short stilts at the bottom of a shallow dip in the ground. Long grass wisped around its base and moss mottled the front deck. A piece of white plastic sheeting flapped from the side of the roof. Wicker matting lay fallen from the front wall, its edges twisted and frayed. It smelled rotten. But as I grasped at the door I realised its handle had been lathe-turned. That's not *so* odd in a school that specialised in craft but I didn't know of any of the older kids who would go to so much trouble about a hut. 'Charlie?' I shouted again. Something about that smooth ball of a door handle made me hesitate. I didn't want to go in alone.

'James?' Charlie cried, uncertain. 'James?' he called again, in a rising tone.

I stepped away from the hut, surprised how faint Charlie sounded, how far I had come. Following his voice through the undergrowth, I finally found him, snarled in a blackberry bush. His baggy blue sweatshirt was trapped in the thorns, his left foot shoeless. He hung there, smiling an anxious smile, looking like the last fat berry of the summer.

'Can we go back now?' he said.

Ben Lyle graduated in Philosophy from Warwick in the mid-nineties. This was a surprise considering it came after an alternative schooling that involved neither homework nor compulsory lessons. He once played football with Bobby Charlton, a lifetime high, and has worked in feature film development for the past ten years.

Tanya Lyn

The Bird

The following excerpt is from the first eight pages of 'The Bird', a story exploring the life of the first female suicide bomber.

I remember the day I started licking my lips. I was almost six and a man in a dirty linen shirt came up to Mama in the alley that led to our apartment. A bright green bird called out and dove into the puddle next to where I sat. The man put money into Mama's hand – I heard it jingle as she dropped it in her pocket. Her eyelashes fluttered, lined with charcoal. She licked her lips though they were already wet. Mama's yellow flower dress clung to her thighs as she disappeared with the man through the thin white cloth covering the doorway to our apartment.

I stuck my hands into the cool puddle and shook the water drops off my fingers.

'Rain!' I sang.

The little green bird flew away.

I wiped the muddy water on my legs. I licked my lips, slowly, the way that Mama did. Then I pulled my bottom lip out as far as it would reach and peered down to see what it looked like. It was pink and didn't look the way I thought a lip would.

Fatima stomped out from behind the white cloth holding a plastic bag of laundry.

'Come, Aya!' Fatima said. 'Mama says it's time to wash.'

I hugged a wadded-up sheet with one arm and traced my finger along the walls slowly through the cracks in the cement and the flaking blue

paint as we exited the alleyway. I imagined that something terrible would happen, though I didn't know what, if I took my finger off the wall too soon.

The street was crowded with date and olive vendors, bicycles, and internet cafés. There were people selling purses on the sidewalk and birds hopping in every direction scouring for leftover nourishment. I saw a large healthy-looking bird bite down hard on another's beak. This other bird was missing feathers and had open wounds on its head. It cried behind its clamped beak but did not fight back.

Rain made the river rise – red from minerals that clung to the rocks. Soon it would be low and clear again. Women washed themselves, their children, laundry and food there. The men bathed further upstream in a wading pool.

The mud from the morning rain was already turning into dust and sticking to my sweat as I kicked it up on the way down to the water.

Some of Fatima's friends were already in the river. She went to them. They all spoke quickly, eyes wide and arms flapping, as though everything they had to say was exciting. Fatima had much lighter skin than the others and her eyes looked like God forgot to put the color in. I set down the sheet I carried on a patch of grass by the water.

Black-necked cranes pecked at the ground a few yards away. I ran to them. Before I reached the birds, a group of boys I had seen in the street by our apartment started throwing rocks in their direction. Cawing reproachfully, they spread their wide wings and flew away.

Three of the boys were tall and dark like the trees on the other side of the river. The fourth, Aamir, was little like me. He was seven years old. We had played together in the street before and I liked him. One of the taller boys spat on the ground. I scowled and threw a rock as hard as I could at him. It fell with a soft thud into the dirt just a few feet away. The tallest boy threw a rock back at me. It hit the side of my head.

Wincing, I rubbed the spot where the rock hit.

'I hate you!' I crowed.

I grabbed the stone from the ground and stomped closer to them to throw it in their faces.

A shower of pebbles and rocks rained on me as all four of them took aim.

'Shouldn't you be cleaning something?'

Thud.

'Lazy mutt!'

Crack.

The stones stung.

I felt them down in my bones as they clunked against my skull and arms, hitting me in the back as I ran away. I fled to my favorite tree, 'Nabi,' I'd named her. She was the biggest tree. I imagined she was the mama of all other trees.

There was a dead bird at the base of her trunk. Flies swarmed over its bloody wings. I walked around to the other side and climbed up about halfway to the top and rested on a branch that was wider than I could stretch my arms. Nabi's leaves drooped in the heat. I lay on my back, heard flies buzzing on the dead bird and people talking over their laundry below.

Then there was a scratching, grunting noise. Aamir clawed up the bark to my big tree branch. He looked down at my face, dragged his arm across his nose and spat a big wad of saliva off the side. It landed with a slap into the mud at the roots. I thought he must want to play.

'Girls aren't allowed to be alone,' he said.

'Fatima is there, at the water.'

I leaned over and pointed to where she washed with two of her girl friends from school. Pink and blue dresses laying white sheets to dry on tall grass.

'You should be washing like the other girls.'

'I helped already,' I said. 'It's too hot.'

A slow breeze clacked the leaves and tickled my skin. Only a few yards away, his brothers stood in a pack. They watched us, nudging each other and laughing.

'Why aren't you with your brothers?' I asked.

'A man can do what he wants.'

'So can I,' I said.

'You can't!'

He straightened his back, narrowed his eyes and flared his nostrils.

'But I always do what I like,' I said.

'You have to do what I say because I'm the man.'

I believed that what Aamir said was true, Mama and Fatima had said

these things to me before. But I did not have a father and had not been spoken to by many men.

He spat again and pulled his pants down. I thought he was going to pee.

'What are you doing?'

'It is not a woman's place to question.'

He lay on top of me in his underwear.

I giggled at first.

He was still for a few moments.

'What are you doing?' I asked again.

Then he grabbed at my dress and exposed my shoulders. He rubbed his face into my chest and made smacking noises with his lips, then moved up into my neck and the sides of my face.

'I can't breathe,' I said.

'Quiet, woman!'

I reached my hands up to tickle him so he would get up.

He jerked my hands off his sides and pinned them down. He glared at me as if he hadn't seen me before. Or like I had done something very bad. I smelled smoke on the wind from cooking fires on the shore of the river. I heard women laughing and linen smacking against rocks.

'I'm cold,' I said. 'Can we play a different game?'

'You're a whore,' he said.

I struggled underneath him.

'You're stupid,' I said.

'And your mom's a whore.'

He squeezed my wrists harder.

'Don't talk about my mom!'

'My dad says so. You're all whores.'

'Shut up!'

I wanted to shove his words back behind his sneer.

'You can do what you want to whores.'

I writhed hard underneath him, squawking strained protests.

His brothers made whooping noises and I heard them clap their hands.

Tears puddled in my eyes.

He stood, pants around his ankles, brow sweating, then wiped his nose on his arm. He pulled up his pants and spat. I felt the tree shake as he climbed down and ran to his brothers who'd begun walking in the direction of the men's bathing site. When he got to them, they all turned

and pointed to my tree. Their mouths wide like the snouts of dogs panting after they've eaten too quickly.

I climbed higher up and hugged a branch tightly until the boys were out of sight. Then I scrambled down as quick as I could. My grasp on the branch closest to the ground slipped. I fell into the red mud, on top of the dead bird. Flies buzzed in an angry cloud. I ran to Fatima with tears in my eyes and mud in my hair.

'Kss! Aya! Why haven't you been helping? You're filthy.'

'Fatima!'

I felt a release of water under my skirt. I shut my legs tightly together to stop it, but the urine dripped into a puddle staining the dust at my feet.

Fatima's mouth dropped at the sight of the puddle. She yanked my dress off in front of everyone. Her friends giggled behind their hands at her outrage.

'Go wash. Now! Stop making more work for me.'

She threw my dress in my face.

I waddled uncomfortably to the river's edge. I put my dress back on and sat on a dry rock with my arms folded, mud drying heavy on my head. Fatima came huffing up behind me.

'I said *wash!*'

She picked me up and dropped my kicking body into the water. She yanked her fingers through my hair until the mud was out.

'Fatima?' I whispered.

She rolled her eyes.

'What, little sister?' she said.

'What's a whore?'

'Kss! Where did you hear that word?' she looked at me the way Aamir had. 'No more stupid questions, Aya.'

She pulled me out of the water. I sensed the eyes of her friends staring at my body as we came back to the drying laundry. There was a heavy feeling, like gravel in my stomach. I tried to cover myself with my arms.

'Fatima!' I said.

I began to cry and dove into her legs.

'I'm cold! I want Mama!'

'Mama is busy. Now be quiet for once,' she said.

Flies flew into the air as Fatima yanked up our dry clothes and folded them.

Shivering, I turned to look at Nabi, tall and strong. At her roots, two mongrels fought over the dead bird that had been at the base of her trunk. I heard the carcass rip and pop as they tore it in half. The dogs gulped down the bird, then trotted upstream, leaving nothing behind but deep gaps in the mud from their claws.

Tanya Lyn, 24, is a writer and visual artist from North Carolina. Lyn has worked in Peru, Papua New Guinea and Israel. She has been awarded the Marion Coe Award for Creative Writing and Dean's Award for excellence in fine art. Lyn has had multiple publications in the *Peel* literary arts journal.

Retšepile Makamane

Testament
Excerpt from a possible first chapter

The door bursts open, hurling in with it the intense morning light. It falls to the floor inside, making a bang more searing than the light itself.

The broken door smashes the fruit bowl. Marbles disperse like mercury, hundreds of shiny particles tumbling haphazardly away from the intruders' feet.

Silence returns. It is as though the men are not walking into the room but floating. Emmanuel suspects that the harsh light is asphyxiating any possible sound, not even breathing can be heard, or the lapping of the river that passes close by, just the whiteness of the light. If he had the option he would ask for a small piece of cloth, a blindfold, a string, just for a drop of darkness. The men file into the room, one by one, forming a line against the inside wall like school choirboys. He recognises their faces because he has been to each one of their houses, and has touched their women in ways that none of them thought appropriate for a stranger. *Makonfane*, as men from the Republic are called in this country. *Makonfane* have to observe a certain distance between local women and themselves. It is an unwritten rule. He finds it easier to keep diverting his eyes to the runaway marbles.

Rolling, rolling, revealing their inside colours the marbles reassert themselves. They regroup into different shades of blue: opal staggers about, unsure. Cyan collides with kyanite and comes to rest. Lapis lazuli is still moving, but languidly, strolling on the lustrous white tiles. All will stop. A

man steps onto a new group forming, rainbow blue from underneath his gumboots peeps. He reaches onto the floor, grabs a handful. The sun makes their edges merge with the white inside of his hand and renders the marbles a cold metallic blue. Angry man. But the man's eyes are a soft caring brown cast towards Emmanuel's hands, fascinated.

The only long-term friendship that Emmanuel has been able to keep in his life is with the marbles. He is twenty-six. The year is 1995. The marbles came from the people his mother used to work for when he was a child. Someone once told him to look very deep into each marble when he felt sour about his place in the world and watch the ocean dance. Therefore, he is familiar with an ocean he has never touched. The TV screen in the corner, next to the last man in the row, is situated on a dark oak room-divider. Emmanuel's picture sprang onto the screen because of the shuffling in of the men which shook the room-divider and the television. He had paused a VHS of one of his services, the previous night, in the heat of love. Now, (his image) caged in between that room-divider, it looks as if he is one of the men standing in the line, readying themselves to judge him against the other him. The him on the futon.

Few drops of blood on his fingers and on the mouth. Sprinklings. He was marooned with an adolescent girl. His loins still burning, like a pervert's. They already thought he was a pervert in any case. 'Twelve!' The women would shock themselves repeatedly down the road where Emmanuel was later paraded. Down the road that passes the colourful Chinese Embassy, which looks like many faraway palaces piled into one building. 'He could not even wait until she was thirteen. Twelve!' Great thing she did not bleed much. Some virgins can soak you red, he thought. He had not been aware that it was already morning. His hands had been full. The whole night. Young love. So fresh – so pure. 'You are pure and new, my own, all of you my own, mine only, my new precious precious Eden woman.' He had said this to the girl every time he zenithed.

The cottage windows face south. The door faces east. The place is also surrounded by pine trees, which make it dark most of the time. Aloof and secretive. The door is always shut. Alas, not anymore. The men have broken the door open like they own Emmanuel's life. As if he owes them rent. He never pays rent. He is an anointed man. He keeps thinking and cancelling out the thoughts: they could have knocked. No. *Kanjani*? That

would have not given them the pleasure of catching me mid-act. Perverted peeping Toms is what they are, he tells himself.

The light. It attacks the interior, exposes their profane nakedness, the girl and Emmanuel on the futon in the middle of the room. Her wenge wood brown body lies tensed against his arm, slightly perched, like a spear-fished barbel that trusts too much in the water to camouflage her. Shocked delicious body of his black Eve. She faces upwards. Her huge afro hides her forehead. Small ripening breasts emit a shining against the sun. Her legs are still sprawled, as though Emmanuel is presenting her to the elders for a virginity test.

The gaping door brings to their nostrils the smells of the street full of wax, tea herbs and the remains of charred paper. The street is heavily scented with wafts of incense smoke coming out of the Chinese Embassy. For the first time this year, the King has permitted the Chinese to remember their dead and manicure their communal graves, at their Embassy down the slope from the cottage. Emmanuel watched them from behind the trees. They burned gifts for the whole week leading to Easter, paper money and car ghosts flaming all the way up to heaven, to their ancestors. They knelt down in deep concentration, clutched their hands together and moved in rocking movements up and down, whispered their dirges and prayers because the dead would come back to revenge their passing on earthlings if spoken to aloud. So they built them miniature shrines and altars next to the tombs for their spirits to dance. To Emmanuel's senses, the incense takes a white smoke Corpus Christi form.

There are six men, each one brought a son. Their replicas. Teenagers. The ones without sons have brought the closest thing to a son they could find. There are in total twelve of them. They want to appear united against Emmanuel, and their wives too, because they know that he knows their lives by now. Their privacies and inadequacies. Men toil the earth as nothing-people until they find women to protect or be ashamed for. The man who infected the colour of Emmanuel's brightest marbles, earlier on, passes the ones in his hand to his son. The man's name is Lefu Shale. There had been a death in the family when Lefu was born, and *Struse God* he has lived forty years of his life burdened by his name. Some said his mother had gone into labour at a funeral, so the flying soul of

the dead relative had recoiled in the middle of the clouds, funnelled back down to the town cemetery and pierced the baby's heart when he was barely out of the mother's womb, and the dead soul resettled. Earth again. At times Lefu would ail for long periods from the dislike of his name. This constant worry had harried his body and form into a gaunt little reject of who he had wanted to be, who he desired and pretended to be in public. For the two births of his children, he had endured worse morning sicknesses than his wife M'e Shale. He chews hard on the matchstick in his mouth, and then shoots a javelin of spit out of the door frame.

The marbles in the son's hands start to transform their colour, back to a place called Recognisable. Lefu settles his chest, assesses the situation, studies the room briefly, says nothing, but takes out a clean and ironed sepia brown handkerchief from his shirt's front pocket, straightens it out and places it on ... he pauses (to take a good look at the girl's *cake*). At least that is what Emmanuel thinks. Lefu on the other hand only thinks of his own daughter who although young, is much older than the case at hand. His daughter is fourteen and has played Scrabble with Emmanuel on several occasions and giggled like a woman to words from Emmanuel's mouth no one else heard. But what is more disturbing is how his daughter has only recently stopped bathing with the bathroom door open. Has this monster touched my child is what he is thinking as he plans to cover the girl. Then he slowly places the square cloth between her legs with both his severely delicate mahogany hands, as if the girl has no choice but to be concealed only there, like an ancient maiden. This act sequesters Emmanuel, leaving him alone and lost in his nakedness, an Adam's grandson. He wishes for a cloth to protect the straining veins in his corneas. He can only place a hand on his forehead to prevent the horizon where the sun just rose from sitting on his eyelids, as it is buzzing about like a bee, about to do just that, camp on his eyelids and scorch them. He sits in anticipation of the men's planned choreography, for Emmanuel had once experienced this kind of sudden morning intrusion in the Republic when he was cohabiting with Rose of Sharon; the day Rose of Sharon was murdered.

Lefu opens the door to the bathroom, walks in slowly, whistles an old hymn – stops. He stands by the sink for a moment, to ascertain that the twelve men in the other room are all looking at him. The girl looks into

the empty space between the walled-up men and the futon. Emmanuel licks the girl's hymen blood from his lips, as it is drying out and causing an irritating itchy sensation. The girl – Qhosha – is a member of the youth choir at the Voice of God church where Emmanuel preaches. Lately, she has been wailing during services. Lefu washes his hands in full view of everyone. Pontius Pilate, Emmanuel thinks. He returns. The room is settling into a strange strange mood. Emmanuel thinks that if he tells them the truth about this unsavoury sight, it will buy him time to negotiate. 'Ntate Lefu let me explain …' The leader of the pack, Lefu, orders the other men and their sons to cut down two logs of the pinewood, as if Emmanuel's unheard plea was a prompt. Strong mature trees, he emphasises.

Emmanuel whispers that this is his day, *joang kapa joang*. He regrets his refusal to accompany Qhosha to the river the previous night, because she said there is a bad weather coming. Maybe this is what she meant.

Retšepile Makamane was born in Lesotho. She received an MA in Development Studies and Gender at the University of Leeds in 2009. Her short stories have been published in *ITCH Magazine* in Cape Town, and the *Oxford University Press Anthology of African Stories* of 2007.

Andrew Parrott

All The Little Sticks
From a novel

My day kicked off early. Working split-shift set me up for bagged eyes, and that kind of soft-necked sag that I get with under five hours' sleep.

You need to look more happy, said Ji, my Korean manager.

She followed me down the corridor, heels clacking on the wood.

I'm too smart to look happy, Ji, I said.

She smiled. She had perfect teeth. Do you remember the new teacher is coming today? she said.

I remember, I said.

I'd seen plenty of new teachers come and go.

I've heard he's young, said Ji – The new guy.

Great, I said. I entered my teaching room, more of a booth really, let in some hazy light, and fired up my PC. My desk smelled like old fruit juice.

Are you going to wear that shirt? she said.

I'm wearing it now, aren't I? I said – Where else am I going to have a shirt?

Are you going to wear a tie?

I have a tie, I said.

Are you going to wear it?

It's in my drawer. I'll get it in a second.

She remained in my doorway, fiddling with a button on her suit-jacket. Her long, painted nail clicked against the plastic stud in a way that thorned my nerves. I pressed my tongue to the roof of my mouth and clenched my jaw.

So, I said – How do you think I look?
Do you really want to know that?
Sure, I said.
I think you have a big nose, she said – And your hair is like a boy's.
I meant my clothes, I said – My hair is like a boy's?
Yes. Actually, it's overly long for you. You're too old to have it like that.
Should I change my nose too? I said.
No, she said – It makes your face look smaller, so you should keep that, but maybe you should get some of the lines taken off your forehead.
I'm only thirty-four, I said.

The computer desktop chirruped into life. I clicked up my schedule and winced. If there were any wrinkles on me it was because of her fully booking me all the time. She watched me from the door.

So you're saying my nose is big enough to make my face look small? I said.
Yes, she said – It's quite fashionable, even though you're old.
How old are you? I said.
I don't really think I'm going to talk about that, she said.
What are we going to talk about? I have a student in two minutes.
She cancelled, so we have time, she said.
She cancelled? I said – What the hell am I here for? I could be in bed.
Yes, she cancelled just now. Anyway, I need to ask you to work longer this morning.
I can't do it, I said.
We have a woman that wants a lesson from eleven until twelve, said Ji – She specifically asked for an American.

There was no way I could have another hour on, especially in the morning. I'd skipped breakfast and run to get in on time, because it's Fucker's Law that the one time you're late the seven o'clock student will actually turn up for class. I pressed my empty stomach. It piped soft, pained grumbles beneath my palm.
I'll do it, I said – If you tell me your age.
She sighed. I'll ask Francis, she said.

My ten o'clock was with Kim Yoonchul. I'd had classes with him before, and he'd always come across as quiet, friendly, pretty strait-laced.

He wore trendy glasses and hair gel and rubbed his forehead a lot. But today he seemed different. His collar lay flat, unbuttoned, and he slouched.

I've been to a party, he said.

What were you celebrating? I said.

He didn't respond. Instead he scootched his chair close and said: I drank a lot.

What was the reason for all the drinking?

Just a party, he said.

He stank of soju. I usually only got drunks at oriental New Year, and that was understandable with the amount of office parties people had to attend. There's an art to avoiding those.

What are we doing today? he said.

Well, we've got a business class now, I said – So we're going to start at chapter four, where we left off. Do you want to recap?

You're speaking very fast.

I guess I am, I said – Do you want to try a business role-play?

Sure. I'm happy.

Good, I said – Me too. Now, I'm going to be a potential buyer, and you're going to be a shoe salesman. We're at a sporting goods exhibition.

What am I doing?

Selling shoes. And I'm buying them.

He nodded. He was sweating beads that mottled on his brow, but I could see he was trying. I couldn't just tell him to go home.

Ok, I said – Sell me some shoes.

Why don't you ... buy my shoes? he said.

They look like good shoes.

They are, he said – They are the best shoes for your feet.

Wow. I like that, I said – They're pretty expensive though.

Why do you say that?

I just wish they were cheaper, I said – I'm going to have to think about it.

He frowned, and said: Why won't you buy my shoes?

I just need to think it over.

Buy them.

I can see you're going for the hard sell, I said.

All The Little Sticks

He raised his hands above his head, arms straight. The tail of his jacket lifted with the stretch. His chair squeaked as it swivelled, and rolled back a pace, so that his face seemed to float away from me. Then he made a chopping motion with both hands. Three chops, a chop for each word: Buy my shoes, he yelled.

OK, I said – We're going to finish the role-play there.

OK.

He dabbed his forehead with a handkerchief.

Were you pleased with that? I said – Did you think it went well?

It was so-so, he said – Nothing special.

I thought it was pretty special, I said – Highlight of my morning. I laughed, but he didn't join in. He was looking at his hands.

I think I drank too much, he said.

What were you celebrating again?

My wife left me.

That doesn't sound like much of a party to me.

It wasn't a party, he said.

He rested his hands on his thighs and cleared his throat. The gesture was easy to read. He had closed himself off. That's the problem with a job where you have to make people talk, where you probe and test and try to make fun. You chip away at them. Without intending, you end up asking too much.

I'm sorry, I said.

I flirted with the idea of not going back to my apartment, of braving Seoul, hitting a restaurant and going to see a museum or something. But my body screamed for rest. I went home, crashed on my bed, and slept with the curtains open. A passing fruit truck woke me. The sellers mount a loudspeaker on their rides, and set a tape to chant their wares.

Orangey, it droned – *Gyul. Subak han tong ey, oh chunan.*

It didn't disturb me too much, and I thought I could drift back into dreams, but then another truck arrived – this one a scrap collector.

Kohjangnan, it hailed.

I'm awake, I said.

Computer, TV ...

I hope you crash into each other, I said.

I got up, set a kettle on the stove, and made a huge brew of coffee. It was an efficiency apartment, so I sat on my bed to drink. After that I went in my bathroom cubicle. The clothes washer, shower, and toilet all inhabited one tiled space with a drain in the centre, which meant I could throw my clothes into the machine as I undressed, and get the shower warm while I took a piss. I felt like a genius.

I walked back to work. The sun was beginning to squash into the haze, looking like a fallen tangerine. The way its beams struck metal on the windows brought out angelic glows. Wind carried a thick, gummy heat with it, and stirred up the dust of building sites along Gangnam mainstreet. To the horizon on either side were brown five-storey lots and dirty-white high-rises, and in their deep shadows the streets became night-blue before the sun had fully set.

My first work of the evening was an assessment. The student was a girl, college age. She was hunched on a grey sofa in the waiting room, frowning at CNN.

Minyeong? I said.

Yes.

This way, please.

I strode through the corridor where all the vacant classrooms were, unlit and unopened, until I came to the interview booths. In here, I said.

The girl bit her lower lip. I entered the room first, sat behind the desk, and waited for her to sort her big purse and coat. Three walls were glass, so I could still see the line of empty coves across from me. Their blinds were strung shut and stationary, the aircon off, the doors locked safe. Through the nearest set of slats I saw a flower on the wallpaper. It seemed a charcoal black in the light, embossed there like a dark eye, taking me in.

So, I said – Have you studied at any other English institutes?

No, she said – This is my first time.

Well, we do mostly one-on-one classes. They're pretty similar to this really, we just sit in a room together and talk. What do you do?

Sorry?

Do you go to university?

Yes, I go to university.

All The Little Sticks

Do you live near here? I asked.

I live near Gwanghamun with my parents and one brother, she said – I grew up there.

Cool, I said.

Where are you from? she said.

I'm originally from the US, I said – Michigan.

Ah, I want to go to there.

Don't bother, I said – There's nothing to see.

She grinned, and stuck the tip of her tongue between her teeth. I marked down some general points, and then moved on to conversation skills. We talked about her childhood.

When I was … when I was young, she said – There were … brogs?

Frogs?

I'm sorry?

I drew a frog.

Ah, she said – Frogs. You paint well.

Thank you, I said. I made a note on pronunciation.

She said: There were frogs nearby my house. I would … catch?

She made a scooping gesture.

Yes, catch, I said.

I would catch, in a jar … frogs, she said. She made a small length with her fingers. But small, she said.

Baby frogs?

Yes. No, smaller.

Poles? I said – Tadpoles?

Tadpoles?

I drew a tadpole for her.

Ah yes. What does it mean? she said – The name. What does tadpole mean?

I had a hard time working that out myself. I cleared my throat and said: Well, tad is an old way of saying small, I think, and pole can mean stick.

Little sticks?

Sure, I said – I guess they're little sticks.

She thought about it for a moment, and laughed. OK, she said – I would catch, in a jar, tadpoles.

You'd say: I would catch tadpoles in a jar.
OK, she said – I would catch tadpoles in a jar. Right?
Yes, I said.
When I was young.
Yes, I said – Cool.
And I take ... took them back to my room. Secret.
Secretly, I said.
Secretly, she said – Yes.
Cool, I said. I made a note.
But I forget about them, she said. She looked away for a moment. My father, she said – Noticed a smell.
Noticed a smell?
She bit her lower lip. Yes, she said – He found the jar. It was very old.
OK, I said.
He strikes me, she said. She tapped her head with her palm and paused, as if expecting some correction. But I'd stopped thinking about teaching by then.
Go on, I said.
He took the jar, she said – I was angry. I said to him: But they have not ... they are not frogs.
I nodded.
I didn't know they couldn't, she said – I thought that after he threw them away, they might still be frogs.
You didn't know ...?
Yes, she said – I didn't know they were dead. They had died.
Wow, I said – That ...
Yes, *that* they had died, she said – All the little sticks.

Andrew Parrott is twenty-three. He grew up in North Lincolnshire, in a village described as a pensioner's paradise. He attended UEA as an undergrad, and taught EFL in Seoul before joining the prose MA. This piece is an extract from a soon to be completed novel.

Joshua Piercey

The Windfarmer
The first chapter of a novel

On the windiest nights the rhythmic shushing of the 'bines blended into a constant white noise that, when caught by a concentrated ear, sounded like the breaking of a single, generous wave. It diffused the howling wind outside the cabin, softened it to a whisper. He had never slept so well as he did on those nights, and never missed his bed so much as on those when he had ridden out to the farthest edges of the farm and spent the night there, huddled inside a weighted plastic tent, the horse swathed in blankets and blinkers to protect it from the cold and the sand. The dust lifted by the wind made visibility poor, but occasionally it was clear enough for him to see the lights of Houston far out in the night, and he slept satisfied knowing that he had made those lights, and that he kept them burning.

New sounds stood out starkly to him, and so he heard the truck approaching when it was still far away. He made toast and coffee and wandered the house barefoot. By the time he looked to the window the horizon was already marked with rising dust, a hazy wedge with the truck at its narrowest point. He continued dressing, only stepping outside when the truck's engine coughed itself silent. The day was brighter than he expected, and he stood on the porch, squinting against the glare, as the sheriff unfolded himself from the driver's seat.

– Got your stuff. And I picked up your mail, too.
– Thank you.
– It's OK, said the sheriff, lifting a large plastic crate from the bed of the truck, – you just stand there on the stoop. I'll do all this lifting on my

own. Lord knows you're busy. Where would sir like me to put all this?
— Porch is fine.
— I got all the usual stuff, 'cept there's no fresh milk this time out because I didn't have the time. And that Chao guy from the distribution precinct says that they're switching out of the last of the original grids and getting the others synchronised, so if the lights all go red for an hour or so tonight then don't bother calling it in.
— OK.
— You need anything else out here? I don't know when I'll be making the trip again.
— I'm fine.
— OK then. Here's your letter. Don't fall off the horse.

The sheriff swung back into the truck and gunned the engine. It grumbled its way past the back of the house, and he stood and watched it until the dust took it from view.

The letter was marked with the stamps of four different postal services. He turned it in his hands, staring out across the plain. The day was cool, a little cloud inked red above the horizon, and the breeze smelt clean. He relished the scent; the air was not often so pure. The seasons were less distinct than they had been when he was very young, although they were better now than they had been twenty years previous. It was cooler, too, and the skies, when they could be seen, were bluer. He stood smiling to himself, listening to the hum of the 'bines, until he remembered the letter in his hands, which was now crumpled and damp. He recognised the measured, discrete capitals of his son's writing. The letter told of progress in the water purification project, and he felt proud that his son had seen to be part of the betterment of the world. When he had finished reading he smoothed the letter out against the flat of his thigh, and then carefully quarter folded it. Later, when the horse was absently grazing and his lunch was over, he would unfold and re-read it, taking his time.

He was on his way back to the house when the flash caught his eye. A sharp glint of sunlight on metal that hovered just below the horizon for a second, and then winked out. He stood loosely still, his arms folded, straining his eyes. The flash returned, in the same place, but lasted only

a split second this time. He waited for a minute, and then two, and then three, but the flash did not come back. He slowly raised his thumb to his mouth, and bit off a rough spur of fingernail, still gazing across the farm. Then he turned calmly but deliberately on his heel, and spat out the piece of nail against the farmhouse as he moved towards the stable.

He talked to the horse as he rode, explaining to it the substance of his son's letter. He did not quicken the animal's pace as it lumbered along amongst the scrub grasses, allowing it to find its own way, but always with the same spot fixed in his eye line. After he had ridden more than two miles he let his gaze drop and began to correct the horse's path. His eyes scanned the ground and he whistled softly, wetting his lips from time to time. After a while he stopped whistling and hummed instead, more for the horse than for himself.

He saw it from a long way off, the only splash of real colour in the sunbleached wash of desert. He slid off the horse and squatted next to it, letting the horse wander away to seek a grazing place. He stared at it for a while. It was a soda can about six inches around, the treated metal still shiny and new. He picked it up by the rim, holding it between two fingers as if unaware of its function and wary in case it suddenly detonated. When he up-ended it a single drop of orange liquid fell out, leaving a tiny dark crater on the sand. He dropped the can back on the ground, and then stood up. Looked up at the 'bines, twirling softly high above. The wind was light, but constant. The can lay in a slight dip, less than a few inches deep. He prodded it with his foot. It rolled away a little, then rolled back. He waited for a long time, until the wind blew harder, gusting viciously around his back, but the can still did not move. So he crushed it as small as he could manage with the heel of his boot, slipped it into his pocket, and whistled for the horse.

A few days later one of the red diodes began blinking, and so he began to tidy and shut up the house, lowering solar shutters over the windows. The house stood almost in the centre of the farm, a low, squat building of dark wood and sheet-metal. On the few clear days it became almost painful to look at as the solar panels bolted to every flat surface drank what they could of the weak sunlight and spat the rest back. The

farm itself extended a half-day's ride in a ragged circle around the house, bordered to the west by a rocky rise in gradient that would eventually drop into a canyon, and to the south by a dark scar of asphalt that had once been an Interstate. The oldest turbines, the ones that had been in place since before he was born, were mostly arranged close to the house, in a loose wedge running to the south-east. The newer turbines were linked to a board of cheap coloured diodes that normally flared a steady green light at all hours. Now one of the lights was dark, and its partner was flashing an angry red. He took some water and all the spoilable food from the fridge, and packed it in a plastic container along with his plate and a water bowl for the horse. Then he shut and locked the front door, leaving the house dark save for the steady green glow and one red star blinking.

By the time he had packed his tool bag and fed the horse it was almost noon, and so he spurred the horse on at a greater pace, occasionally patting its neck and apologising for the hurry. Every so often he would sing aloud, continuing until he embarrassed himself by straining for a note out of his reach. He used the 'bines to orientate himself, working his way through the numbers printed half way up the shafts, a few feet above eye-level. It took nearly three hours to reach the one corresponding to the winking red diode back at the house. As he drew close to it he noticed a dark stain on the ground, less than a hundred yards away. He stopped the horse as he came up to it, but he did not dismount. It was clearly the mark left by a fire, a raggedy circle of ash and debris too regular to be anything other than human in nature. He stared down at it, and pulled at the reins sharply when the horse bent its head to sniff at the ground. After a time he urged the horse on towards the broken turbine.

He dismounted and tethered the horse to the tower's shaft with a long rope. The curved blades were more than thirty feet up, and the horse had long since ceased to be bothered by the twirling white paddles that rose all around. It rumbled at him until he absently stroked its head, and then it ambled away. He stared up at the turbine. It was still turning steadily and quietly, and he listened for any creak or irregularity that might indicate fatigue, finding none. The three blades were still perfectly

shaped to catch the breeze, curving round one another and joined at both top and bottom to one arm of a three-pointed star. It looked to him like the guard of some ornate sword. He stooped and spread his toolbag, removing a sealed plastic box and a torque wrench. He used the wrench to remove carefully the bolts from a metal panel at the base of the turbine's shaft. When the last bolt was gone he prised off the panel and leant it against the shaft, then prised off the rubber seal around the opening and put it in the plastic box to protect it from the sand. The mechanism inside was still in motion, although the indicator light on the dynamo was out. He reached up inside the turbine's tower to apply the brake. When the blades had stopped revolving he opened the panel on the dynamo, flicking the rubber switch to ground it. One of the ceramic plates inside had smashed: he would need largely to disassemble the dynamo to replace it. He worked steadily for two hours, frowning to himself. Periodically he stopped, turning to stare over at the blackened smudge of the cold fire.

When he was done he smeared the rubber seal with petroleum jelly (although lightly, for the pot was almost empty and the stuff was precious), then bolted the metal panel back on. Then he began to set up the tent by the dead campfire, letting it unfold and inflate as he poured water for the horse. The ash and dust left in the sky meant nightfall always came quickly, so he pooled his own supplies with what was left of the charred wood on the ground to start a fire of his own. He stared into it until the night was truly dark around him, then put the blanket on the horse and crawled inside the tent.

In the darkest hours of the morning he stepped out to piss, naked save his boots and his wristwatch. As he urinated, fidgeting against the cold, he stared out into the night and watched the little orange speck of another campfire, a few miles away. He looked at it for a long time, until the cold became unbearable. Then he swore softly to himself, and fled back to the tent.

Joshua Piercey studied English Literature at UEA. He is currently working on his first novel, *The Windfarmer*.

Rob Magnuson Smith

El Pensativa

Down in Buenos Aires, after receiving a diagnosis of advanced lung cancer from a team of implacable physicians wearing neckties, I took a taxi to the Museo Nacional de Bellas Artes in an effort to calm my nerves. I was in Argentina as a visiting professor of metaphysics, on sabbatical from my university in the United States.

It was a hot afternoon in January. A discarded newspaper on the floor of the cab announced the record temperatures that had been afflicting the region for weeks. As my driver rattled his way through the Recoleta District, the cafés stood empty, the streets deserted. Packs of sleeping dogs filled the sidewalks, giving me the impression that I'd already begun descending into the underworld. As we passed a florist, I lowered my window for air, only to recoil at the mounds of dead flowers that clogged the gutters.

Finally we turned onto the wide thoroughfare of Avenida Libertado, with its parks and trees. In the distance a couple kissed under the shade of a cypress. At that moment I plunged into the terrifying sadness that continues to dominate my remaining hours. I hadn't expected to die at forty-seven. At the same time, I couldn't exactly take issue with the diagnosis. I'd played a game of chicken with my lungs and lost. My final days on Earth would be defined by a suddenly incongruous desire to live.

The museum appeared abandoned. At the top of the steps, the doors had been flung open, as if the patrons had fled an inferno. Even the concrete benches by the entrance looked buckled and misshapen by the heat. I came into the lobby. A handful of security guards slumped

forward in folding chairs, sweating through their white uniforms, breathing in shallow gasps. They looked constructed out of stone, like the terracotta warriors guarding the tombs of Chinese emperors.

I visited the Museo Nacional on a weekly basis. I liked to refresh my favorite paintings in my mind and pay them mental visits during a wait at the post office, a sleepless night, or a tedious dinner party. Despite my patronage, the clerk checked my coat, as always, without recognizing me. I realize that my appearance is forgettable and drab, that I have led a largely inconsequential, academic existence. But that afternoon, after hearing the lurid laundry list of my coming symptoms, I would have appreciated a familiar nod.

I headed to the Italian impressionists. I sat alone on a wooden bench and faced Antonio Mancini's portrait of the beautiful grieving woman, *El Pensativa*. An electric fan in the corner swept hot air across my ankles. My eyes blurry, my feet damp inside my socks, it seemed the walls were dripping with humidity, the paintings melting in their frames. I went through the stations of my life's journey, now accelerating to an end – the scholarly appointments and conferences, the childless marriage, the carefully planned, yearly vacations now merging into a single indistinguishable blur. Soon, I kept thinking, I would be joining the ranks of all the other departed professors of metaphysics, each as faceless as the last.

The *Pensativa* leaned against her sofa in a black mourning dress. Her ashen face floated in the center of the painting like a moon. She fingered a silver cross on her neck, one eye facing out, the other drifting sideways, as if to recall a memory. The right half of her mouth rose while the left sunk downward. I wished I could be taken into her gaze. I wanted to be disembodied, transmuted into the elements of her expression, incorporated into the very oils on the canvas.

Art has forever pestered me. As a strict philosophical materialist, I've spent my professional career debunking concepts like elegance and grace. The so-called masterpieces, after all, are merely configurations of paint. Neuropsychology demonstrates that the elements of romantic love reside in the interconnections of the hypothalamus. Altruism is a form of social learning. We may call a complex collection of notes a symphony, but its harmonies are reducible, its effects contextualized, its

mysteries eliminated by the proper analysis of each musical phrase. At least these are the positions I used to hold. I make no apologies now – except to say that I was mistaken.

Years ago, I was offered a window into a more enlightened plane. I had a glimpse of the ineffable and turned away. Perhaps the most crucial moments of our lives are necessarily threatening. We escape with our easy choices, close the synapses, harden the arteries.

I had been driving across America. I had left my university in the East for my graduate school in the West. Only twenty-two, I'd begun publishing early drafts of my airtight, materialist arguments and had been offered fellowships at leading doctoral programs in metaphysics. In the town of Marysville, Kansas, I stopped to stretch my legs. While walking Main Street I passed a one-story wooden structure called The Museum of the Pony Express. The entrance fee was only a dollar, so I paid and pushed through the turnstile. Strewn across the counters, old shoeboxes held an assortment of ephemera. Soon I came across a black-and-white photograph of a female sharecropper in a torn dress. She stood at the edge of a wheat field and scowled at me with a determination to survive. She fixed me in her haunted gaze.

For nearly an hour I stood unable to move. Against all reason, I became convinced that this woman had been waiting for me inside the shoebox, that she'd called me off the highway and into the museum to bear witness to her hardship. Surrounded by cracked leather saddles, a replica of a Pony Express stagecoach, and walls covered with canvas mail satchels, I fell under the spell of a person long dead, and therefore very much alive.

Who allows a photograph to undermine his philosophical convictions? I never once spoke of my experience in Kansas, nor allowed it to infiltrate my professional papers. That day marked the beginning of my descent. Not long after, I developed my nervous compulsion to chain-smoke.

While I sat on the bench reflecting on the Pony Express Museum, the *Pensativa* kept her right eye on me. I've always thought she regarded me with pity. 'I'm dying,' I told her, though I suspected she already knew.

I turned to make sure we were alone. It is embarrassing to be caught speaking aloud to a painting. I wondered how Mancini had created such

a beautiful portrait of devastation. Artists must be clinically delusional to believe their works might one day succeed. They start their projects with nothing but ideas, knowing the critics and the philosophers are waiting to pounce.

The *Pensativa* didn't reply to my confession, of course. I tried to focus on the right side of her face – the gleam of romantic reverie, the moist, upraised half of her mouth. Instead, I kept returning to the side that tilted downward, to the wrinkle in her wayward eye, as if to find a reflection of my own advancing grief.

'Remember me,' I asked.

The fan in the corner blew dust at my shoes. I heard a creak above my head – among the pre-Columbian artifacts, someone was browsing the centuries like so many department store windows. I needed to get home. I hadn't yet told my wife the diagnosis. She'd had no idea, when we first met, how diligently I'd been withering inside. Now I was loitering in a museum, unburdening myself before a portrait of another woman. I pictured my wife at our kitchen table, her fingers encircling her porcelain teacup. She was preparing to interpret my blank, colorless face.

I shared a final moment with the *Pensativa*. Then I stood up, somewhat lighter on my feet. An American couple crossed in front of my bench. 'It's strange,' the woman said, stopping to study the painting. She clutched her husband's wrist. 'You get the feeling she's trying to communicate to you.'

'That's just what art does,' her husband said.

The woman took her camera from her neck and pointed it at the *Pensativa*.

'Make sure to get one in black and white, honey,' the man advised.

Soon, my photo will appear in the obituaries. You'll see me in the back of the newspaper, a dead materialist staring you down in my suit and tie. But I left a truer image of myself in Buenos Aires that afternoon – hands clasped, eyes closed, listening to the camera click.

Rob Magnuson Smith was raised in England and Oregon. His debut novel *The Gravedigger*, winner of The William Faulkner Award, is published by *University of New Orleans Press*. Rob's fiction has appeared in *Inkwell*, *Fiction International*, *The Greensboro Review* and *Notes from the Underground*, and is forthcoming in *The Reader*. He is the 2009-2010 winner of the David Higham Award.

Sunita Soliar

Porsche
An extract from a novel in progress

When Miraya opened the front door she was startled to see Asyel sitting on the stairs, a figure in black against all that slick, white marble. Asyel stared at her, cold and accusing.

'You're late,' she said.

Miraya avoided her gaze and put her keys on the hallway table. The clink they made seemed to echo around in the vast silence. She remembered how airy and bright she had once thought the house. But now it was as if a perpetual rain fell, darkening the furniture, and making everything damp to the touch. And Asyel was always there, waiting to put her back in place amongst her other wet things. The air conditioning blew chilly breath over Miraya, drying her sweat into a cold glaze.

'I'm going for a swim,' she said. 'I'll see you at dinner.'

She headed for the stairs.

Asyel stood up abruptly, stopping her. 'We go now.'

'I want to go to the pool.'

'It will wait.' Asyel walked to the hallway table and picked up her car keys, looking forcefully at Miraya.

'Asyel, no.'

Asyel appeared to consider. 'Please,' she said. 'You come with me. I want to go somewhere. It won't take long.'

Miraya felt it might be dangerous to refuse her. 'All right.'

Asyel walked outside and got into her Range Rover.

'Where are we going?' Miraya asked.

But Asyel was already starting the engine and did not seem to hear. Miraya got in. Asyel sped through the gates, scarcely waiting for them to open fully, and drove, jolting and swerving down the road. She trespassed into a neighbouring lane, forcing a cyclist to jerk out of her way. Panic leapt into Miraya's fingers as she gripped the armrest. It was stupid to have trusted Asyel to drive.

She took a sharp left onto Hammersmith Bridge Road. From her window, Miraya, uneasy, watched the bridge pivot slowly as they passed, then her eyes shifted anxiously towards Asyel.

'Did you sleep this afternoon?' she asked.

'I couldn't.'

'But you took something to help?'

She didn't answer and turned onto the A4. Shadows travelled along her arms and cast pallor over her face. Her eyelids drooped twice, swaying the car. Miraya wondered, with dread, how long ago she had taken the pills. She must not alarm her: at these moments of drugged wakefulness, Asyel was as fragile as when she sleepwalked. She asked, as evenly as possible, 'Are you sure you don't want to tell me where we're going?'

Asyel's voice was distant, hollow. 'It's a surprise.'

Miraya hadn't paid attention to Asyel's appearance when she came back to the house. Now she took in all the little details of her: the black décolleté dress, her backcombed and lacquered hair, her large teardrop diamonds. All at once there was something ominous, something inexplicably wrong with this.

Half an hour later the motorway turned into tree-lined roads in Berkshire. Asyel bore down a country road, the trees on either side tall and oppressive. It was quiet at that time of night, and only two cars passed by. Miraya looked about her searchingly, but she saw only place names that had no meaning to her.

Asyel turned onto a bumpy dirt road. Ahead Miraya saw a large Italianate villa set behind gates. Several flower-beds and a large fountain ornamented the forecourt. Asyel slowed as they approached, and turned right. She leaned over Miraya and peered through the window. Following her gaze, Miraya saw Alexis's Porsche alongside a black limousine.

Sunita Soliar

Asyel parked. She fiddled with the charms on her bracelet. 'You knew,' she said, her voice a whisper. 'You knew.'

'Asyel, I –'

'I wouldn't have believed it but then this!' She reached into her handbag and pulled out her mobile, pressing buttons. She thrust the screen at Miraya. It was Emin's latest music video. On a beach, winking at the camera, Asyel's husband, Emin, crooned his lyrics: 'your lips so fine, your smile divine.' And there was Alexis, dressed in a bikini. Emin rolled about with her like a kitten with a ball of wool. Miraya looked at her hands.

Asyel said, 'He even put her in his video. You knew about this too?'

'I didn't.'

'Look at it.'

Miraya did not want to.

'Look at it. I wouldn't have believed it but see the way he touches her!'

Slowly, Miraya looked: there was no mistaking the feverish passion. She said, 'I'm sorry.'

'He's in there with her and it's your fault.'

'Asyel –'

'It's your fault. I hate you. I'll never forgive you. I hate you!'

She reached her arms out to scratch Miraya or hit her, pushing forward with the force of her whole body. Miraya grabbed her wrist, wincing as Asyel jabbed her nail into Miraya's arm. Asyel's other hand pulled Miraya's hair until she let go. They grappled.

'Stop this!' Miraya said. 'It isn't my fault.'

'You should have done something.'

'Why? I'm just someone you keep around so you can ignore the fact that your husband treats you like shit!'

Still holding on to each other, they froze. The words were out there between them, filling the space of the car.

'It's not true.' Asyel could only whisper, and tried to strike her again. Her fists were weak and Miraya let her hit out until she was still.

Mascara rolled down Asyel's face like tar. 'We came here once. It is quiet. No one finds us. I knew he'd bring her here.' She paused, considering if she should ask the next question, unsure if she wanted to know. 'So this is Alexis? The girl you're supposed to be keeping out of trouble?'

Porsche

The car seemed small and stuffy, Miraya's skin clammy. 'I should have told you.'

Asyel twisted a charm frantically, her fingers trembling. 'But it's ridiculous. She's a child. She's —'

'Alexis is a stubborn brat.' Suddenly the wrong struck Miraya personally. She wanted to defend Asyel. 'It's a game to her.'

Asyel blinked as though something sharp were coming towards her. 'I feel stupid. If Emin saw me, if they saw me —' She broke off, her inflated cleavage sagging under the weight of her sadness. 'I thought maybe I would go in and say something, that I could make them ashamed. They are laughing at me. Or probably they are not. Not now. But when she goes to smoke a cigarette or whatever she does, she will be laughing at me.'

In the dark, all dolled up in that dress, her lipstick smudged and those black rivers moving down her cheeks, she looked like a faded marionette. Miraya squeezed her hand. 'Come on, let's go home.'

They heard the wolfish growl of Alexis's Porsche speeding out.

Miraya touched Asyel's arm. 'Let's wait a bit, eh?'

Asyel stared ahead, fiddling with the key. Then she started after the Porsche.

As they drove out of the private road and onto the tarmac she accelerated. Miraya nervously watched the needle on the speedometer climb. On either side trees rushed past them. Ahead there was only the red Porsche, illuminated by Asyel's headlights, and endless night that thickened and deepened as they advanced. Asyel darted forward, swinging towards and away from the kerb, close on Alexis's tail. Alexis stuck her hand out of the Porsche's window and gave them the finger, surging ahead. But Asyel had no intention of being left behind. She ignored the lanes and cut the corners to keep up, as they wove down the country roads.

'What the hell are you doing?' Miraya yelled.

Asyel ignored her. The Range Rover almost touched the Porsche's bumper, then she relaxed her black stiletto from the pedal. When there was a breathable distance between the cars she pressed down again on the accelerator, and lurched forward.

Too shocked to speak, Miraya stared at Asyel: speed was her whole

menacing being. She was alone and focused only on that patch of colour in front of her. Alexis thumped the horn in desperation but Asyel paid no heed and worked the accelerator hard to keep up.

Miraya reached for the wheel, but Asyel shielded her away with her elbow.

'Stop this!' Miraya yelled. 'Right now!'

Asyel swung into the lane for oncoming traffic, nudging the front of the Range Rover alongside the boot of the Porsche.

Miraya grabbed the wheel, yanking the car to the right. Asyel fought her for it. For a moment their eyes met. Asyel tried to look away but that ray of human contact brought her back. She eased off the pedal, allowing Alexis to pull away.

Perhaps she intended simply to move back into the correct lane, but she veered too early, and her car clipped the Porsche's back wheel. It swung to the right, spinning around, its tyres screeching, and flew headfirst into a tree.

A wail that sounded to Miraya like buzzards rose. Suddenly she realised it was the Porsche's alarm going off. She noticed that the Range Rover had stopped moving. The bonnet of the Porsche was crushed against the bark. A leaf fell onto its roof. A fly fretted around the windscreen wiper of the Range Rover. A piece of fluff floated above her leg. These things pulled her away from the ugliness outside and drew her into the small space of her seat. She could stay there, inside these little things.

Gradually a different sound, a cry of some sort, called her back. She did not want to know what it was but it went on, drawing her out from the fluff, the fly, and she was forced to recognise Asyel crying 'no, no, no,' over and over again. Miraya was afraid to look at her, afraid of what it might mean. But she felt her head turn in little jerks until she saw her. Asyel's hands were still on the wheel. They shook as she stared through the glass, the trinkets on her charm bracelet swinging.

'Jesus,' Miraya said. 'Jesus, Asyel.' Numb, she opened her door and stumbled out. 'We have to do something.' She spoke more to herself than to Asyel. 'We have to see if she's OK.'

Asyel didn't move: she fixed her eyes ahead of her, and took feeble

breaths.
'Come on,' Miraya said.
'Emin. What will Emin say? I didn't mean to –'
'We have to do something.'
'If Emin finds out –'
Miraya exploded. 'We might have killed her!' She leaned into the car. 'Do you understand? Do you understand, you crazy bitch?'
Miraya's fingertips were yellow where she steadied herself against the dashboard.
'Fuck,' she said, slamming the door. She walked the few steps to the Porsche. The distance seemed so far, the road underneath light, insubstantial. She looked through the shattered window. She couldn't see Alexis's face because of the airbag. She did not want to touch the car, but slowly she reached out her cold fingers, and tugged at the door. It was jammed. She walked around to the other side, but it was too close to the tree. She would have to get help quickly. She went back to the Range Rover and got in. Asyel stared at her. Something about her expression, nervous and helpless, brought back the girl that lay under all the heavy painting. Miraya could almost touch her: her Asyel, her friend, only fear had drawn its nails across her face.
Miraya reached for her mobile. 'We have to call an ambulance.'
'They will see the number. Then Emin will know.'
Suddenly, Miraya understood what she was asking her to do.
'Asyel, we can't just leave her there!'
Asyel only looked back blankly.
Miraya turned away, but her own words, jumbling themselves with Asyel's, rang in her head. She closed her eyes and held onto the edge of her seat. Outside the trees wavered in the dark.

Sunita Soliar was born in 1983 and lives in London. She studied the International Baccalaureate, and has a Masters in English Literature from UCL. She is a regular short story writer for a quarterly newspaper, *Fitzrovia News*, and has also been published in *Notes from the Underground*.

David Strickland

The Whisper and the Whale
An extract from a novel

The Oldest Man is one hundred and six years old. He lies up there inside his room, the oak door is battened down, the lamp is almost burnt. Everyone in Chuchote can feel his going. It scuffs over the largest stones and whispers along the lake. It rumbles across the wooden boards of each of the chalets in the village. A few weeks ago, when he could still stand, he dragged his huge feet around the bed; his head almost brushed the ceiling. 'No more now, get out,' he said and the villagers closed the door and left. And then they stood on the stairs and imagined him inside, feeling in his pocket for that secret twist of tobacco. Chewing it slowly as he looked out at the mountains.

His mouth has opened, he lets out a breath. An old person's breath goes further: it can fill a room with gentleness and grow steam on the window panes. It can race right out of the door. Eloise hears his breath turn into a choke. She waits a little longer outside on the path in the cold, looks up at the light in the window and pushes a wrinkled hand under her bonnet, warming it against the grey curls of hair.

There are many stories about the Oldest Man. Some say his father's father was brought up by wolves in Chuchote. Others that he was kidnapped as a child: whisked away by a rich Vicomte, to live in a château near the coasts of Provence. When he was well, Eloise remembers how the children clambered around his legs and tugged on his sleeves, asking for stories about when he was a boy. But he would never tell. 'Here and now, all that matters!' he would shout. 'I could have come from a donkey!' He would always make them laugh, kindness sweetening

authority, so that they came to feel easy around him. Now that he is sick, the village has become quiet. No one asks for stories anymore.

Eloise moves over to the door. Even with the light of the moon above her, she cannot see well through the dark. She reaches up and rests her hand over the letters and numbers engraved in the stone: *LAVARRE 1648*. Here under this same lintel, the villagers pass each week and congregate in the back room. They gather together and hush themselves to a listen as she teaches them the rules of the New Faith.

She lifts the heavy black knocker in the shape of a hand. Lets it drop against the wood. Then she pushes the door open. Inside, she steps up the wide staircase: the echoes from her feet sound like a slow clapping. She grazes the top of the baluster with her fingers, brushes a line in the dust. She will talk to Lisette about cleaning and tidying later on. To make the dying a little easier, she thinks. As she reaches the bedroom door she stops, out of breath, and looks up. The steps spiral on through thick beams of pinewood to the small attic room at the top, where she and the elders meet in private. She thinks of what the Oldest Man could want. A blessing maybe. Some holy guidance. She still feels the need to impress him. Even now after all these years. But then, when she steps inside, she forgets everything else.

The room smells strange. The Oldest Man lies in his bed, his feet dangled helplessly over rolled-up blankets, his arms pushed through a cream nightgown. Lisette Duprés stands over him, squeezing milky water out of a cloth into a shallow bowl. When she sees Eloise, she sweeps across the room and kisses her on both cheeks. 'Go home,' Eloise says to her. 'I will take care of him for a while.'

'Much better today,' Lisette says and then snaps the door shut after her.

Eloise sits down. The Oldest Man grips the sheets in his fist and smiles, his huge face gathered up into a crease.

'Ah,' he says. 'Our little Eloise.' As if time has turned its tail by fifty years. Eloise, the child, newly arrived in Chuchote. Standing there on the path, holding her mother's hand.

'You look tired,' he says.

She almost laughs. This man, worried for her, making an effort, raising his voice to its full loudness as he lies with his legs in the air, dying.

She moves her chair closer to the bed. 'How are you?' she says.

He stops for breath. Coughs into a wet hand. Looks up at her as if she should understand. 'You are going down to the valley more,' he says. 'Be careful of it.'

She does not ask him why. The thread of life in him hangs so gently, she cannot disturb it. He sneezes suddenly and she feels it like a burst of wind. It takes him by surprise and he groans and then laughs until his throat gurgles. His skin turns a little pale.

'A messenger came up here on foot,' he says. 'Two days ago.'

'From Baleine?'

'Yes, from there. Sent by M. Le Maire. He asked about Last Rites. Said there are still three priests working across Aquitaine.'

She says nothing. Such a thing, so strictly against their faith.

'I said no, Eloise. I said that I have you.'

'The Book of Truth is clear,' she says quickly. 'These rituals are pagan.' She hushes herself. So clumsy, disrespectful.

She tries again: 'I pray every night, Fabrice, that you will see the Paradise when God sees fit.'

'Ha!' He coughs and laughs at this. Lays his great hand on hers. 'Nothing we say comes right when we talk of death. It is a slippery thing, Eloise.'

He raises a finger: 'I am not gone yet.'

After he falls asleep she sits beside him a little longer. An uncomfortable feeling comes upon her as she watches over him. She glances sideways at her own mortality. Imagines gasping that final mouthful of air. Her body placed inside a wood box and dropped into the dark mouth of the Chute that plunges down to the valley below. To dust we will return. It makes her shiver to think of it. She would not be with her husband now; she would have to lie in the earth alone. His body would be buried somewhere else. She realises that during these past weeks she has been thinking of him more. Not the memory of Auschgang disappearing. Rather the ghostly shimmers of him fumbling sardines from the shelf, or sitting at the step of the door, playing a concerto with a small blade of grass. But then she brushes these thoughts away. What selfishness when the Oldest Man lies right there beside her.

'You will be fine,' she says out loud to him. 'You were built like the mountains.'

And then his eyes fall open, caught between waking and sleep.

On the way home, Eloise crunches over the gravel. Her ankles swallowed up by mist. The few houses in Chuchote, passed down the generations and strongly bound to the grass, disappear for a moment. She must find her way quickly: Antoine will be waiting for her. She walks on past the precipice to where the path separates. Then, to her right, she finds her gate swinging open.

As she walks into the house, she sees Antoine. He sits in the chair by the fire, unable to hide his shivering. His young lip holds the beginning of a moustache. Then she sees his cheek, black and a little blue, as if he has pulled himself out from under burnt wood.

'You have something,' she says and brushes her finger against the bruise. Then watches as he turns away from her.

After she has boiled tisane for them, he begins to talk. He brings up what has happened in his eyes, the fight leaping out in the reflection of the last embers. He tells her that he went out late. To collect kindle. He was walking over the hill, with the mountain behind him. When he crossed the path that led down to Bigorre, he came upon them. At least thirty men, a few metres away in the dark. They were quietly wrestling and beating each other with pokers and sticks of fire. Antoine could hear them breathing. He tells Eloise it must have been a border struggle, a fight between the villages of Artouste and Béon. As he glanced over he saw two boys he recognised, standing some way from the others. He had been to school with them in Baleine. They watched as he walked past them, but neither dared stray off to take him on themselves. Then a flaming torch came flying out towards him through the air. It hit him just below his cheekbone and fell to the ground.

'I did not turn round,' he says. 'I kept on walking.'

Eloise feels her eyes grow wet. He looks straight at her now and then looks away and says quietly that he is sorry.

When Antoine first arrived from the valley a few weeks before, he did not speak for days. His mother, Vivienne, had begged Eloise to have him stay, just for a while. Some mountain quiet, she said, so he can have time to think. Eloise had wanted to know him then, she had hated the delay, it was like a book with stuck pages. And slowly, as he talked, his future became her all-consuming aspiration. It warmed and worried her to sleep. It still does. She stares at his bruise once more and says goodnight.

And then she whirls away, out from the room, swept along by her worries.

A lake perched in the mountains is a strange and temporary thing. Fir trees grow close around the water, as if fearing it might disappear. But the lake still survives. It has taken each person's voice, each quiet testimony, and given it a place to rest. In the early morning, the light not yet risen, Eloise sits with her knees squeezed to her chest, her feet close to the edge of the water. She listens as the wind gasps through the branches above. Thinks of the times with Auschgang. Before they married. She came here with him day after day, during the winter months. They followed the earth path that danced down the slopes towards the forest and when they reached the lake they hid in the bushes, still laughing, holding their breaths so as not to see the steam rise from their mouths. He would turn to her suddenly and say 'fruit feast,' and right then they would race each other along the water and rip balls of mistletoe berries from the trees to feed each other. She rubbed them in his beard and dropped them on his tongue. Not too many though, she rationed them carefully so that he never felt sick from them.

She keeps waiting for him now. Almost as if he might appear at any moment beside her. She has been waiting for him ever since he left. Wondering if one day he will need her help again. She stands up, feels a light breeze mutter on her arms, looks out at the green water. She comes here often. It is like this, alone, by tipping your head back and letting the loneliness soak into your hair rather than turning and struggling away, it is like this that things can continue calmly.

She hopes never to meet anyone out among the trees, on the same paths before dawn. She, the one who has tempted God back to Chuchote. It would not mix well with quick-spread stories of an old woman stumbling madly around in the dark. So she treads lightly on her way back home, and though she has never seen a man or woman awake at this time in the morning, her boots do not crack a single twig.

David Strickland was born in London and has lived and worked in Paris and the South of France. In 2009, his writing was shortlisted for the *Biscuit* International Short Fiction Prize. He is currently working on a novel about love and fundamental religion set in a remote village in the French Pyrénées.

Anastasia Tsalta

Hotel Royale

It was early in the afternoon when I arrived at Hotel Royale. I paid the fare, got out of the taxi and there it was: Hotel Royale in all its glory. To be perfectly honest, the only royal thing about it was its name. Other than that there was no apparent reason why someone might be reminded of kings and palaces when looking at it. Location was one of the main reasons, I suppose. According to the brochure, the hotel was within walking distance from the nearest metro station, and in a picturesque part of the city. According to my own eyes it was in a dead-end alley. I had been advised to take a taxi instead of walking there. For safety reasons, I suspect. It wouldn't take a genius to realise that this was a fine example of what journalists call a 'bad neighbourhood'. In the sky above me, I could barely see the sun. I could barely see the sky, for that matter. All I got was a glimpse of fluffy, dark red clouds. The alley smelled of gas, sweat and garbage. A stray dog barked at me as I neared the entrance. I was standing right under the shadow of Hotel Royale. It wasn't tall, only six floors high, slightly dilapidated. It was surrounded by taller, impressive buildings that made it look even duller, if that was possible. I couldn't help noticing the hotel's neon sign. Only the letters H, E, L and L were still in place. The dog was still barking at me. I entered.

I was surprised to see that the interior was in better condition than the exterior. But still, that wasn't saying much. I announced myself to the receptionist. It was a boy. Blond. He had recently cut himself shaving, judging by the tiny bits of toilet paper stuck on his cheeks.

– Mr. Lipern isn't it? We've been expecting you. Please sign here and

here. Perfect! Your room is 6C. Please, follow me, this way. Oh, is that your luggage? Allow me.

We entered the elevator and he pressed the button to the sixth and last floor. It was an old-fashioned elevator. An unbearably slow wire cage lift. Made me feel dizzy.

We finally reached my floor after six minutes that seemed to me more like six hours. There was another man in the corridor. The ugliest man I have ever seen. He looked at me, with his huge, goggle eyes and muttered something unintelligible as we stood outside room 6C.

– Don't mind him, sir, he is just the cleaner. He is not from around here.

He took a golden key out and unlocked the door.

– Here you are Mr. Lipern. This is your room. Nice view, huh? It's one of our best rooms, if not the best. We only give it to special guests, just like you. In case you need something, anything, press button 7. Hope you enjoy your stay here.

I tipped and he left, closing the door behind him. I was feeling terrible. I had spent the previous day at the airport. My flight was to have left the previous morning. It had been cancelled. Just like any other flight. A volcano, somewhere in the North, had erupted and as a result I was now stranded in this city. You see, the ash extracted had been deemed too dangerous for planes to fly through. I'd desperately tried to find a jet to hire. Nothing. Nada. I'd just wasted my time at the airport. Anyone I asked told me the same thing over and over again.

– Sorry, sir, but for the time being no one is flying. Still the situation is dynamic and subject to change. Why don't you book a room and phone this number every six hours? It's much better than staying here, at the airport, tired and restless, don't you agree?

Anything was better than that noisy and filthy place. The problem was that by the time I began searching, all the hotels had been fully booked. Apparently, I wasn't the only one affected by the situation. The only room I could find was at that two-star hotel. Needless to say, it came as a shock to me.

I am, or I was, a financial advisor. A very good one. The best amongst the best. That meant that I was used to luxurious comfortable suites in five-star hotels. Being in Hotel Royale was a huge change to my lifestyle.

I dropped on the bed. My head was spinning. I reached into my pocket and took my pill box out. Opened it. It was empty. I remembered that I had taken my last sleeping pill two days before and I had been planning to get new ones as soon as I got home. Those pills, they were very strong – I needed to get a prescription from a doctor first. Something told me that it would take a long time till I had the box filled again.

I was tired. I was uneasy. I was anxious. I was supposed to be on the exact opposite side of the globe right now, attending a meeting. Far from here. Away from this disgusting alley. People depended on me. They were expecting me. I called them, of course. Told them everything about the volcanic ash, how it had affected me, how I could do nothing about it. They weren't pleased. They didn't express that directly to me, but I could tell. After all, analysing was my job.

All I wanted to do was leave. All I had left to do was wait. All I needed was sleep.

There was a TV in my room. The channel reception was terrible, though. I either got image but no sound or sound but no image, but never both.

There were some DVDs as well. I had to choose between *Deppie's Wet Adventures* and *A Day in the Life of the Reproductive Termite*.

I was losing it. Nothing inside that room, nothing in the entire world could help me.

There was a Bible on the night stand. I wasn't the religious type, thank God. Underneath it, there was a notebook. I opened and read it. I really had nothing better to do.

The name Ctesylla was written on the first page.

The second, third and fourth pages were torn. Tuesday 13th: Meeting with EX 08: 50 p.m., Hotel Royale, room 6C. The rest of the page was blank.

On page six the following was written:

I woke up early today. EX was already gone. He'd left a blue rose on the nightstand and a note saying how much he loves me. I went to the bathroom and then I found out. My reflection was gone. I looked all over the bathroom mirror. Zilch! I immediately opened my purse mirror. Nothing there either. I looked for it in all the mirrors of the hotel. Zero results. My reflection was nowhere to be found. None of the other guests had seen it. The cretin that is the hotel's cleaner claims that he caught a

glimpse of my reflection in EX's motorcycle mirror. The receptionist advised me not to pay any attention to the cleaner.

– That man is a liar as much as he is scrofulous. But there is no one in the whole world that can deter dust like he does. That's the only reason we keep him around. As for your situation Madam, on behalf of the hotel management, I deeply apologise for your misfortune. I suggest you leave your contact details, so we can inform you, in case your reflection is recovered.

I asked him, my voice trembling, what were the chances of me getting my reflection back?

– I can't really answer that, can I? People tend to lose the most amazing things in hotels. Only last week, a gentleman claimed that he had left his conscience in the bottom left drawer of the closet in room 6C. We checked, but there was nothing there, apart from camphor tablets, of course. He was persistent and he demanded the entire hotel staff be searched. None of us was found with an extra conscience. That gentleman – he is a judge – left our hotel without his conscience. I am not a nosy man, but if you ask me, I think that it was that young man who followed him up to his room. I had never seen him before and never saw him since. He came with the judge, stayed for three hours and then left. If you ask me, I think he did it.

I suggested going to the police. Maybe they could be of some help.

– You can always try, why not? They will file a report, and promise you that they will get your reflection back. But they won't, they never do. Finding lost reflections or consciences has never been their priority. Trust me, I know them too well. This one time, a girl and her father were guests here. In room 6C. In the middle of the night, the girl, she was six or five I believe, started screaming, accusing her father of robbing her of her childhood innocence. I was on duty that night and I called the police immediately. They arrived two hours later, took statements and left. The next morning the father and the girl left as well. I never found out if she ever got her childhood back from her father. I am only saying this to warn you. Policemen, they just don't care. But you can always try.

I don't care what he says. I will report the loss of my reflection to the police. I called EX. He wasn't answering the phone. I left him a message, asking him to call me back. I know that he will. For the time being, I

must find a way to survive without a reflection. I found writing to be particularly useful. By writing everything down, I feel more concentrated and can easily reflect on things. Until I get my reflection back, because I know that one day I certainly will, I will use this notebook as often as I used my mirror purse. Until then ...

I finished reading there. Besides, there was nothing more to read. The rest of the pages were either blank or torn. I gazed at the painting that hung on the wall. It depicted a battle scene. Men on horses attacking the fortified walls of a city. I felt my eyelids get heavy. I tried to keep them open, but it was impossible. I fell asleep.

Ever since then, I can barely keep myself awake for more than one hour. I just can't. I don't even know what day it is today. I can't keep track of time any more. I cannot even tell what day it was the day I arrived. Maybe it was Sunday, maybe Monday, maybe Tuesday. But I know for sure that I arrived and I am certain that I will leave this room, some day. I've called the airline company so many times. They said that the ash cloud is spreading, that I should wait.

And that's what I've been doing.

Waiting.

Sleeping.

Dreaming.

The clouds on the sky above get thicker. My dreams get more intense. Sometimes I dream of playgrounds, where adults are forbidden; other times I dream of a pure and just world, where the impious are punished. But mostly I dream of Ctesylla's reflection. I know that one day I will wake up for good and as soon as I check out, the dreams will desert me. But I can't help wondering which part of me will be left behind the door of room 6C.

Anastasia Tsalta was born and educated in Athens, Greece. She studied Communication, Media and Culture at Panteion University before coming to UEA.

Vicky Warren

Cliff Failure

Unseen and far below, the tide was coming in when Julian pulled over on the cliff-top road. He turned the engine off and wiped condensation from his window. The grass expanse hadn't seen a mower since summer. Isolated benches faced the horizon over a fence dotted with scrub and waste bins for dog poo.

'... Till after your tea, and not before.' A woman's voice sliced the wind. Its owner walked past him along the pavement to a café door a few yards to his left. She put her bags on the ground and unlocked the café.

'Two minutes!' she called back up the hill before disappearing inside. He watched a boy run down and throw himself over the handrail, blue coat swaying in the air, arms and legs dangling from either end.

Julian had an hour of daylight left. This time of the week he was always in his office. It felt strange. He pulled out the key and let his thoughts race till thinking made him feel sick again. Brambles shivered against a sky blotched with grey. In the silence of the car a thin whine leaked out. He ignored it. The sound came again. Claws clattered on the plastic mat, and the suspension wobbled. The car was his wife's. He hated it.

'Be quiet!' he said.

He unclicked the seat belt and turned round.

'Christ! Look at the smears on that bloody glass.'

He wound down both front windows. Cold air ripped through, took the warm tang with it. Socks and old chicken flesh.

'God, you stink!'

He opened the door and stepped out, zipped his coat and walked towards the cliff. Fifteen strides away the precipice was shut off by lines of fences, newest at the front. Rusted, wind-wrenched, the man-made boundary was retreating as the rock crumbled beneath. The outermost defensive lines were broken but no one had taken them down. White plastic rectangles swung squeaking from the fence here and there, cracked and faded. Only the word 'Samaritans' was still legible, above a ghostly image of someone with a phone.

Heeling forward the dog dragged Julian down a zigzag path, eyes goggled with effort. They turned at the bottom onto the concrete promenade. Its rampart curled in like the stern of a ship to meet the cliff where steps led down to the beach. 'Danger! Keep back, – ' said the sign overhead ' – These cliffs may crumble at any time.' A pigeon moaned in an old sewage pipe which jutted out from the broken crag. Julian unhooked the lead. The dog pitched itself down the narrow stairs and bounded stiffly across the sand.

The cliff wall towered overhead, a landscape sliced open. The rock lay in two strata – white above, red-brown under. He remembered his geology suddenly, how what lies beneath will come to the surface somewhere, and he tensed, feeling the cut of the cold. All along the beach at the base of the cliff lay rubble in heaps, vast slabs of chalk poised at steep angles, like a glacier slide frozen in motion.

A man in a cagoule bent to gather pebbles or shells. An old couple ambled along the wave-line in big coats. Julian pulled his zip up to his chin and skirted close to the cliff to avoid them, passing a slope of stones ten foot deep along the base of the rock. Not a random arrangement, but a smooth form, all white like a heap of fist-sized sugar granules. A valley of red stones dipped in the middle, dividing the chalk. The rocks couldn't just have arrived at that shape. It was unnatural. He bent and picked up a palm-sized lump. He hadn't been here in years. The swell curled its lip, and sighed as it broke. Seagulls bobbed on the waves out beyond the breaking line, every head turned in unison to face the wind. He thought about the people in the town, how soon they would find out what he'd done. How they would hate him. He wondered what his wife was thinking, checked his phone.

'Where's that stupid animal?' he said.

He straight-lined the route his dog had looped, eyes up scrutinising the cliff-top for stands of brush. Way ahead, a retriever bounced round a collie. He whistled to it. All around, black rocks rounded by centuries of sand and tide lay like sheep, weed-coated, their heads and limbs tucked under while the ocean slowly drowned them. Up above a stand of thorn bushes curved backwards from the cliff-top as if a storm still blasted. The retriever ran with the collie now, following another man. It wasn't Julian's dog.

He turned back.

From this angle he saw the blackthorn against the sky. Boiled and twisted, it stuck out from the thin soil, clinging by one root to the air. A single concrete post stood beside it and three more of the same hung free from the ground suspended by the fence. Far below, two juggernaut chunks of rock tilted up their broken sides.

The beachcomber walked a circle on the sand, eyes down, arms cradling something. Then two brown eyes and a blond muzzle looked at Julian over a boulder and vanished.

'Skippy! Come here!' he yelled. Then under his breath, 'Bloody idiot!'

Nothing came. There was no way to get to the dog except by scrambling over rocks like an eight-year-old. He found a foothold.

'I wouldn't do that if I were you.'

Halfway up the pile Julian looked round. To his right the beachcomber stood on the sand in front of the strange arrangement of rocks, white smears all over the front of his cagoule. He sounded Scottish, looked Julian's age.

'Didn't you see the sign?'

'I know,' said Julian. 'I live here.'

The man bent down to the pile of rocks at his feet. 'There's a rotten seal in that hole where your dog's hiding. Has been for a fortnight.' He wiped his hands.

'What are you doing?' Julian looked again at the thousands of pieces of chalk. 'Is this an art thing?'

'Art!' The man stood at the base and lobbed a lump onto the top of the pile. It clacked, and sat where it had landed. 'No. I'm reinforcing the cliff. Stopping it from falling over.'

The next piece was red. It landed on the red section and rolled down into the white. A gull traversed the cliff-face, broad-winged. Its screech echoed, faded as if resigned. 'So this pile of stones you've made – it's going to beat the sea?'

'That's the idea.'

Julian started to laugh, but stopped himself. 'What about storms? How long is it going to last when the waves are eight feet high?'

The man crouched and took a rock in each hand, then tossed both at once, collected two more lumps on the back swing and threw again till the stack at his feet was exhausted.

'It gets halved generally, at the worst. We have about four big storms a year, although there were three last spring, and two in the summer. But I give it a few hours a day, and I usually get everything back up within a fortnight. Some people help. Add a stone as they pass.'

The man wiped his nose with the back of his hand and said, 'There hasn't been a fall along my stretch since I started. So – you never know. And it keeps me healthy, anyway.'

The dog was a dead weight as Julian dragged him to the sea by his collar. The man shouted, 'Anything that makes a difference, eh?'

The day was coming to an end, like the last pages of a book. A text beeped. Julian's wife: 'Away sister's few days to think. Took your car as you weren't back. Look after Skippy.'

So that was it. From the cliff-top path Julian waited for a last view of the sun as the planet rolled away into evening. Pongy mutt! How disgusting would you be to her if you were a man? A mile away a beam of light shone out of the cloud onto the sea, a beneficent gleam on one of a million indistinguishable khaki waves. He rubbed Skippy's neck. Skippy looked up and closed his eyes, used to being touched.

In Julian's mind this was where they remained, at the earmarked spot above the dead blackthorn, even three hours later, at home, having done everything that was necessary. Julian had pulled the dried flower display out of the hearth to light the fire. The dog lay on its side and absorbed the heat – features blank with stoicism. His tail thumped the carpet when patted, belly full of fresh beef. On the coffee table Julian's supper tray held the other steak from the pack of two – half-eaten, over-cooked

Vicky Warren

among cold chips. He had got closer to finishing the bottle of wine, the most expensive one in the supermarket. It was musty. He suspected it had been on their shelf for months. At midnight he woke on the sofa to a scream from the telly. The fire was cold. Skippy stood beside the table, head jolting as he gulped. His wide flat tongue licked across Julian's plate, made it bang and slide.

And the tide was out again below the parking spot on the green when Julian returned two hours before dawn. The night was wide and calm. But it wouldn't last. He'd laid out the letters at home and the office, and soon the first person would arrive for work. Traffic would come onto the streets and walkers onto the beach. Not even this moment would be his anymore. And he had nothing else.

He heard a van and lifted his head off the steering wheel. His forehead hurt. The rear-view mirror was a lozenge of neon street lights, leaden apartments, brown sky. All around the car, grass and fences, thorn bushes and signs seemed erased. He had been through the options, round the same rut. And now he saw the darkness was splitting in two. A jagged line defined the land's end in front of him. He started the engine, and let it run till it was warm. He felt the injustice, the air solidifying round him like a prison and then he stamped the accelerator into the plastic mat and held it down as if he could push it through the footwell. He gripped the handbrake, the steering wheel, revs climbing. He smelled the smoke. Not loud enough. A dog's head popped up in the mirror, turned in silhouette, ears raised. The engine note screamed to its peak. He held it there, brake lifted and then released the force. The purple bubble leapt forward like a baby goat, threw itself into a downhill gallop. Over open ground and into the first wire. A jolt as the car smacked, thumped over a post that smashed and groaned along the undercarriage. His head was tossed against the A-frame. The yards multiplied, seemed to stretch apart into the possibility of failure. But now gravity reached out where the little engine faltered, gripped and drew down slow, slow, fast over the final feet like a playground slide – unstoppable. Crashing sounds gave way to silent flight, then another whine, high and sustained as the heavy dog spun into the back of his master's head, and slate-blue sky ripped up out of sight.

A police cordon closed the cliff and beach all morning while the area buzzed with vehicles and uniforms. Fire crews and an ambulance, coastguards and community support officers unravelled the wreckage of man and dog, car and rocks. The tide came in behind them and harried their work, wiped the tyre tracks, erased the footprints, washed away the shards they were too slow to find. And when in the afternoon the rock man came back to mend his stack he noticed no difference, just a few stones out of place.

Vicky Warren is writing a novel about a disastrous colony and a psychotic sea captain. She lives in Norfolk with her husband and two children.

Eleanor Wasserberg

Lie Still
The prologue to 'Foxlowe', a novel in progress

In the attic room at Foxlowe, Freya eyed the distance from the bed to the door. She burrowed a veiny hand up to the top of the quilt and fingered the heavy chill air. Then reached further up, to grip the iron bedstead. Cold shot through her fingers and the joints there twinged. Ashen light poured sluggishly from the window. She shifted her hips to angle her sight to the brass keyhole. The light streaming through it flickered. The Something was moving.

Freya imagined the journey to the hen house outside. She broke it into pieces, so that each was too small for fear to catch hold. To the door – always seven steps. The descent into the main house – a hundred or so, down the staircase. Through the ballroom and the hall, another hundred. Twenty down the servants' steps to the kitchen, a dozen steps across. The garden, fifty, on grass. She closed her eyes. Just lie still, lie still. But it had been days, maybe weeks. The hens would be hungry.

Her nightdress caught on the mattress as she stood, and Freya looked down at herself. Spindly legs sticking out of something her grandmother would have worn. She swayed with memory-vertigo. She was older than her grandmother had been when she died. 'It's horrible,' she said aloud. She looked around the attic, the low ceiling, and the window onto the moor. She pulled a strand of dull hair around to inspect it. 'Horrible, Foxlowe,' she said.

Freya lurched forward defiantly. She counted, and there the door was. She grinned. Her mouth tasted sour. She put her cheek to the clammy wood. The Something that had been crouched outside seemed to have

evaporated. With an effort, she bent to peer through the tiny tunnel of the keyhole. The narrow corridor was full of wintry light. She could see the top of the banister. A cobweb spanned the space between the carved finial and the banister slope. She steeled herself and tried the door. No weight. Freya let out a breath. She turned the worn handle until it clicked, and stepped out with her hands hovering in front of her.

On the staircase, the hair on her arms prickled, and she lost count. She froze on a middle step, stooped to sit. Better to be still. She looked at her bare feet. There was a butterfly tattoo below her left ankle, faded yellow buried under a white film of skin. A hunger cramp swelled and died within her. Freya tilted her head to one side, remained still. She strained to catch the Something.

It had begun as a ripple that she sometimes found at the corner of her eye, in the garden or while she navigated the staircases. Then it scratched across the roof when she was in the upstairs rooms. It squatted outside the attic room at night. For some time it pressed against the door there, making it too heavy to open. Freya wasn't sure how long she stayed up there, lying on the bed, telling herself she was tired and needed to rest. *Just lie still, lie still.* Think of a story.

The crackle and tingle of Freya's ears was like dead air on the radio. There was nothing now except the low hum of the ley line. Rob's fervent voice came to her, from the first days of the commune. *The old pagan current runs right through Foxlowe, a direct line to the Roaches on the moor.* She pressed on to the hallway. The panelled walls still smelled of beeswax.

When she reached the kitchen, she wrinkled her nose at the smell of rancid damp. She stepped into the huge boots that sat against the Aga and slid the bar lock back across the door. She regarded the soggy garden. Grey fog drenched the moor beyond the Foxlowe border. Freya stroked the door frame for luck. Her hand flaked away some of the paint. She pulled a coat over her nightie, then trudged down the railway sleeper steps, until a plummeting weariness made her sit on the last block.

'Tired, aren't we, Foxlowe,' she said softly. She dug at the blue flecks of paint that sat in the crust under her nails. She smoothed fingertips over the rings entrenched under her knuckles. Over the last few years,

Foxlowe had aged with her. The creaks of the settling house began to sound painful, like old joints. The walls lost their strength against the world outside.

Over the garden, a hen squawked. Freya hauled herself up. Mud oozed from under the frost crust when she eased onto it from the last sleeper. A childish impulse seized her and she tried to stamp across it. She managed to weave her way, enjoying the squelch of the ground as she went. She thought about taking off the boots and letting the cold mud seep between her toes. The girls would have liked that – her Laura and Joanna. They would've laughed to watch her now, in her nightdress and wellies with a parka over the top, stomping in the mist.

The land that belonged to Foxlowe was marked by little boulders. The founders had laid them as though they lived in the centre of a stone circle. Now the overgrowth covered the stones and the garden bled into The Lane that led to the Churchyard and beyond that, the moor. The Lane was now a mass of nettles and brambles that Freya hadn't crossed for years. When she wanted to get onto the moor, the carer had to drive her back through the town to reach it from the other side, through a new build estate.

Freya unstuck her boots from the mud and tramped to the edge of The Lane. She peered across it, on tiptoe. On a clear day you could see as far as the Bridestones and the sharp tips of the Roaches. Today The Lane was covered in the hanging wet, like suspended rain. The fog came right up to the old Foxlowe border. Freya dared herself to reach out. She knew that there was old salt ringing the house. It kept out the bad from the moor and the barrows. They would scatter it every solstice and New Year's Eve. Freya squinted into the grey. Something shifted out on the moor, a cloud within the cloud. She stepped back, her arms at her sides.

'No matter,' she said obstinately to the fog, her chin raised. She didn't need to see the moor, she knew it by heart. To the west was the hill called The Cloud. At summer solstice you could stand at the edge of the Churchyard off The Lane, and watch the sun set twice. It disappeared behind The Cloud, and then set again on the further horizon of the Cheshire Plain. Freya had watched it every year since the first solstice she came to Foxlowe. They'd all gather in the Churchyard and drink hot tea and moonshine, while further down the moor, the Roaches and the

Bridestones flooded with the fading light.

This year, Freya had missed it. The carer had promised to take her down to the edge of the Churchyard, the only place it could be seen, but he was late. She sat in the garden, raging, watching the normal sunset. When the carer arrived, she spat on the floor of the hall and wouldn't let him in. She ignored all the letters that followed, in their shiny council envelopes. A few weeks later the Something slipped into the house.

Freya braced her back against the hen house door, then kicked a weak spot until it gave.

'Hello old things,' she called out as she entered. 'Sorry it's been a while.' There was a low throaty sound, like a chuckle, from one of the hens scuttling forward, and as Freya fell like a block of ice, she had time to register the blood on its beak.

The crouching Something, the weight against the door, had become sharp, a pinprick of heat that ignited somewhere near her temple. The only thing to do was lie still until it passed. To not be afraid. But it was harder outside the house, without Foxlowe, without the walls and the hum of the rooms. Freya couldn't raise her arms to swat away the darting movements of the hen, Maggie, around her cheeks and hair. The hen house dimmed. Looking at the wall, she knew the fog now pushed against it. One summer the girls had painted it yellow; the drips were still visible. Joanna's hair had stuck together with paint, and Freya felt again the pull of the knots as she teased it out.

The pinprick started burrowing like a parasite and the hen house wall disappeared. Freya saw her own face in a thousand mirrors, always with the same colourless eyes. A glimpse of herself pressing her eyelids, to see the colours that she could make in the black space. The spot rummaged deeper, to where her mother's voice was kept locked away. *You have the most wonderful eyebrows, I have to pluck mine, where did you get those from?* It was before Foxlowe, in their old kitchen, her mum's hands cupping her face. Freya stayed there for an endless time, until Foxlowe tore through the scene, the first time she saw it, the light behind the house, the gardens at sunset, then her first solstice and many others all jumbled up into one memory, the weight of a child in her arms then the girls at her side as they grew, different dresses, and their shivering in the sudden blackness, waiting for the sun to reappear on the far plain. The

Eleanor Wasserberg

heat found and burned up long lazy nights with Rob and other long forgotten friends and enemies, herself smoking and arguing, but most of all watching Rob's mouth.

Her hand, motionless on the straw, felt the thousand other hands it had held. Laura's hand, smooth and cool, stayed longest, and then it was gone. Freya waited for the Something to find Joanna. It brought her girl, ripped and bleeding, her last painful summer. The last thing Freya saw before the blackness was Joanna lying stiff and burning in the attic room, and herself curled up around her, saying, *Just lie still, lie still. I'll tell you a story.* Joanna's silence, the slow cooling of her fevered body. Then Freya uncoiling herself to look at Joanna's face and a long moment of something falling, from her throat to the pit of her stomach.

Outside, the fog shifted and moved in. It rolled over the garden, through the slats of the little house. The hen, Maggie, scratched and scratched.

Eleanor Wasserberg was born in 1983 in Staffordshire, where her novel *Foxlowe* is set. She was awarded an Arts and Humanities Scholarship from UEA. Before coming to UEA, she read Classics and English at Oxford, and taught English in London and Paris.

D.W. Wilson

Ballistics

Part One: Chance

'Having seen a small part of life, swift to die, a man rises and drifts like smoke, persuaded only of what he has happened upon as he is borne away.'
Empedocles

Alan

On a Friday evening in September, not too long ago, a friend of mine spilled a bottle of lager over the cedar coffee table in my living room and slurred her curiosity about how it all began, that summer I spent in a scour across the Kootenays. She doodled her finger through the caramel froth yeasting on the table's surface. I thought about getting a paper towel, but I thought about a lot of things. How it all began – well, we could trace Gramps's defects all the way to his childhood: some shrapnel he blocked with his sternum when he was seven, the result of a dud artillery round on a beach not slingshot range from home; a welding arc that dashed across his chest while he tempted his body's conductivity in the rain; smoke inhalation, steam scalds, stress levels, and a consistent blood-alcohol for all those years strapped in a Nomex jacket, *Volunteer Fire* stencilled across the back in white. That's his history, but if I were to pinpoint the moment when everything Began, the summer my family's history came a-knocking, I say this: at eighty-two years old, Gramps had his heart attack.

It was a poorly ventilated evening in May, the kind of evening that encourages a man to splay himself along a loveseat and wear musked-up muscle shirts from his childhood. Gramps's house offered little in the way of airflow, so we'd wedged the storm door with a Gore-Tex boot and unshuttered the windows, and something like a breeze tickled my pits and the skin on my topmost ribs. Earlier, Gramps had salvaged a blastworn industrial fan from his storeroom, but I lacked the technical savvy to revive a guttered rotary, and Gramps lacked the sobriety. We'd settled onto the furniture in his den to suffer through UFC exhibition matches as we waited for the approaching dark.

I'd only been in the valley a couple days, home from university to finish my thesis and keep my mind off the girlfriend drama that'd driven me there. It was to be the last visit before my indoctrination (a PhD in philosophy). Gramps went to the kitchen and banged open his fridge and I heard him palm a pair of bottled beers. From the couch I watched the dusk light glance off neighbouring roofs. Years ago, Gramps strung a mosquito net abreast the exterior window because brown birds tended to get drunk on the gemstone berries growing on a nearby tree, and they'd kamikaze into the glass. One day he found a family of those birds piled at the house's foundation, and when he lifted them in his palm their necks lolled like tongues.

Pillow clouds swirled above the Rockies and I smelled that pinprick sensation of lightning on the horizon. Wood smoke loitered in the air like breath – it clung to clothes and furniture, a scent like chimney filth, or hiking trips along riverbeds, or the charcoal that remains on a campground after the campers have moved on. The province was in flames. Folks in the interior had fled their homes, and each morning I woke expecting to see the town ablaze. Earlier in the month, the parks had declared Fire Warning Red and everybody – locals and tourists, bluecollars and rednecks, cops' sons, preachers' boys, parlour philosophers, even the old, haggard men who huddle under the pinstripe tarp that sags off the bakery – doused their camping pits and boiled their hotdogs and darted amid traffic to stamp out cigarettes left to smoulder in the heat.

Gramps set the two open beers on the coffee table. On the television, two long-limbed Muai Thai fighters lilted in half-moons around each

other, gloved hands at temples, knees drawing like longbows. Then one of those stick-men split-kicked forward, sailfish-fast, and Gramps made this noise like *ununghf* and I looked over and the old bastard'd gone scarecrow. He lurched sideways and one hand clawed for the end table but fanned it, hauled a circa 1970 lamp down atop him, shade like a hot-air balloon. Well, I'd completed an Emergency First Aid course years ago, so I launched into CPR and dialled 911 and saw the paramedics green-light him for de-fib in the ambulance.

I rushed inside, grabbed Gramps's keys from his hunting vest, and took his Ranger. It was a three-minute drive to the hospital, up a hill with a sixteen percent gradient and then past a rundown hostel with its stink of dope and unwashed thrill seekers. As I crested that hill, driving straight west, I was struck by a clear view of the Purcell mountains. For a moment, under the sunset sky, they looked to be on fire, the treetops glowing red and orange like a thousand heated needles, and it seemed I could see past them, through that shield of rock and carbon, to the very flames that ravaged the province's interior. I felt a gust of warmth in my eyes, like the dry heat from a wood stove, like a welding torch, as if from the blazes burning on the mountains' far side.

When I arrived at the hospital, a receptionist with curly hair sat behind a desk built into the wall on two sides. – My grandfather had a heart attack, I said.

– Cecil West?

– That's him.

She directed me to a carpeted lobby with a window overlooking the courtyard of an old folks' home. There, a double-bent man, out for an evening stroll, passed half a sandwich to a dalmatian at his side. In the room with me, a toddler drooled on a Tonka dump truck he'd filled with alphabetized blocks. He mimicked an engine's hum as the Tonka trundled left to right, where he dumped its cache in a heap against his knee.

Then a tall woman my age, with blonde hair tied in a bun and a thin, square jaw like a boy's, stomped into the waiting room and glared down at the toddler. She wore blue jeans faded in scruffs at the thighs and a grey T-shirt cut above her triceps. I recognized her as a fling from my high school years. Missy, she used to be called.

– Where's your brother, she said to the toddler.

D.W. Wilson

– Went to get a coke.
– And left you here, she said, and looked right at me when she did. Then: – Alan?
– Hey, Missy, I said.
She curled an arm to her hip. – Nobody calls me that anymore, she said, but didn't seem upset. – You all right?
– Gramps had a heart attack.
– Jesus.
– Yeah.
– Don't worry, if I remember your Gramps, he's too stubborn to die.
– Thanks, I said.
She pressed the back of her wrist to her nose, and I thought I recalled her doing that in high school. – You gonna be around long?
– Just the summer. Working on my thesis, now.
She bent to scoop the toddler under her arm, prised a stray block from his pudgy hand. – Got a job lined up?
– Well.
– Danny's a cop. That's my husband.
– I don't remember him.
– You either, she said – a retort, but I'm not sure what she meant by it. She made a 'gotta go' motion with her head.

Outside, in the courtyard, the double-bent man raised himself to height, dalmatian by his side, and together they scuttled toward the care home's backdoor. Gramps had told me, time and again, that he'd rather die than spend his final days locked up with a bunch of blue-hairs. If he got that bad, I was to drive him to his cabin in Dunbar and there'd be a hunting accident involving his trusty twelve gauge. Couldn't do it himself, he said, else he'd get eternal damnation. At least once per visit he and I swung into his game truck – an old four-by Dodge reeking of hides and the rusty scent of bled animals – and drove down Westside Road, past the ostrich farm, to the gravel pits where high school kids built bonfires big as campers, and we'd waste the day and a carton of rimfires on emptied tuna cans and paperback books Gramps had deemed uninteresting at best.

When I was finally admitted to Gramps's room, I found him in an aquamarine hospital gown, upright but bedridden, spotted with sticky

discs and wires that relayed iridescent spikes to a CRT. He shifted in bed. Deep lines drew along the cusp of his cheekbones and wrinkles bundled like metal shavings in the corners of his eyes. He peeled his lips over his gums in what could have been a smile.

– No flowers? he said.

– I only bring flowers for good-looking girls.

– I'm in a gown.

– And it brings out your eyes, I said, and sat on the edge of his bed. He seemed very small beneath that sheet.

– You doing OK? he said.

– What kind of question is that?

He cast his eyes to his hands, fiddled with them in his lap like a man embarrassed. I chewed a hangnail on my thumb. He looked old, too, all of a sudden – moisture filmed his irises and his cheeks sagged at an angle off his jaws, bespeckled and age-worn, and what little hair remained seemed wilted, thin, like the strands you find gummied to the tiles of a public shower. He looked, I guess, like a grandfather on his deathbed.

– I'm dying, he said.

– No you're not.

– It's like approaching a wall.

I nudged his thigh with a fist. He flashed his teeth.

– I'm not just traumatized. A guy knows when the time is up.

– What'd the doctor say?

– It's coming, Alan. I can feel it.

– No. You can't.

– I need you to do something for me, Gramps said in a drawl I didn't like. – And I need you to do it without asking any of your ridiculous philosophy questions.

Then I was outside under the fluorescent lights that lit the asphalt parking lot like an ice rink, and then I was in the Ranger with its smell of Old Spice and sloshed beer and everything else my grandfather. From the radio, a monotone voice droned factoids about the burning interior. I drove the long way around Invermere's lake, like I used to do when I was sixteen and desperate to ogle the girls whose folks had come from Calgary to spend their summer in the great, untamed wild of the

Kootenay Valley. At the beach, kids half my age gathered under a streetlight. They dabbled toes in the water and sloshed whiskey on their gums and I cringed at the idea that kids were now half my age. Home, I went to Gramps's bedroom, like he instructed, and inched a shoe box from beneath his bed. It was maroon and covered in dust and dog hair and inside was a trove of sentimental items: a tarnished cap revolver with a sulphur-scorched hammer stained as though by ochre; a dehydrated poplar leaf big as my hand; at least two mouths' worth of baby teeth, some my own; a wedding band too large for any of my fingers; a silver Zippo lighter adorned with the American Eagle. And there, at the bottom, I found an address with the name Jack West scrawled in my grandfather's blocky script. I ran my fingers along the letters and, lifting the paper from the box, felt the passing of a burden. What goes around comes around, they say, but I'm not so sure. Never really leaves, maybe.

– I need you to find your dad, Gramps said to me from that hospital bed. – Because I don't know how much time I've got left, and there are some things I need to say to him before I go.

D.W. Wilson is the recipient of UEA's inaugural Booker Prize Scholarship. His fiction has appeared in *Malahat Review*, *PRISM*, and *Prairie Fire*, and he won the silver fiction award at the 2008 Canadian Magazine Awards. He's a Canadian citizen by birth and temperament, and working hard on his novel, *Ballistics*.

Life Writing

Introduction by **Kathryn Hughes**

Maddy Tongue
Vanessa Morton
Cassandra Scott
Annabel Howard

Here at Life Writing Towers, we've experienced a bumper harvest of wit, invention and downright brilliant writing. This year's graduating cohort offers a range of lives as disparate as they are fascinating, funny and sometimes downright odd.

Maddy Tongue sets the tone with her study of the woman who inspired Elgar to write his famous 'Dorabella' sequence in the Enigma Variations. When 18-year-old Dora Penny met 38-year-old Edward Elgar in Wolverhampton railway station, she can have had no idea that she was to become the catalyst for one of the most celebrated pieces of music in the English tradition.

Moving to the other side of the country, we encounter Olive Edis, an enterprising Edwardian who made her living as a photographer in the Norfolk resort of Sheringham. Edis did her fair share of hack work – portraits of picturesque old sea salts to sell to tourists – but, as Vanessa Morton reveals, Edis was also an accomplished artist with a sharp and subtle way of capturing her sitters' souls.

Cassandra Scott takes us further away still, to Durban in the 1970s where she gives us an intimate glimpse into what it's like to come of age in a family marked out by its difference. Does having a brother incarcerated on Robben Island mean that you're not allowed to mourn your own childhood? The answer seems to be 'yes and no' in this powerful piece by a former political journalist from South Africa.

Finally, Annabel Howard asks us to look hard, really hard, at the way in which the Emperor Nero's image has been used and abused down the ages. Her point is a big one: why do biographers ignore portraiture as a source of (mis)information about the person they are writing about? It is these kinds of questions, raised here in four outstanding pieces of work, which lie at the heart of what the Life Writing MA programme at UEA is all about.

KH

Maddy Tongue

Elgar's Dorabella: An Enigma of Musical Biography

'Dear Miss Penny: (That's not right)
Dear Miss Dorabella, (That's feeble)
My dear Dorabella (pish! very ordinary)
Now for it - My dear & adorable Dorabellissima, (That will do)
Once more, My very or most dear & most or very
adorable Dorabellissima!'
(Letter from **Edward Elgar** to **Dora Penny**, 15 October 1902)

On 6 December 1895 the composer Edward Elgar met Dora Penny on Wolverhampton Station. It was their first meeting. Elgar and his wife were coming to lunch with the Pennys and Dora was there with her stepmother, a close friend of Elgar's wife Alice. The two ladies had much to talk about so Dora was left to entertain Elgar. She found him informal, easy-going and full of fun. He tried out the piano in the drawing room, was excited that their house was close to the football ground and together they tried to mend a broken chair. Dora was twenty-one, Elgar was thirty-eight. Out of the informality of that day arose a relationship that lasted for nearly twenty years.

Elgar had married Caroline Alice Roberts in 1889. She was nine years older than her husband and described as small and pleasant looking rather than attractive.

Alice was the daughter of a distinguished Major General: her outlook, manners and expectations were fashioned by her place in society. There had been opposition to the marriage: her aunt, appalled that Alice was marrying

someone of a lower social class as well as a Catholic, disinherited her. But Alice was determined. Both her parents were dead and she, in spite of marrying a struggling music teacher with a background in trade, never doubted that he would be successful. Elgar in 1889 was still not an established composer and the couple had little money: he taught violin lessons at the local girls' school and Alice had a modest income of her own, but money was scarce. By 1895, Alice was approaching fifty. Elgar was still full of youthful vigour and enthusiasms and Alice recognised  that many of his energetic outdoor pursuits did not suit her. Dora's account of her relationship with Elgar, in *Edward Elgar: Memories of a Variation*, was first published in 1937 under her married name of Powell. Her diaries, although limited to brief notes, reflect the life she led as the daughter of a Church of England cleric. A typical diary entry reads: '11 March 1896. Went to deadly dull At Home in the afternoon and a still more d.d. one in the evening. A few spots of rain.'

She was twenty-two.

Little wonder that when Elgar entered her life with his charm, his jokes, his music and his love of the outdoors he must have filled it with a vigorous masculinity lacking in the decorous rounds of parish duties. Her familiarity with and love of music gave her an immediate rapport with Elgar. He made her laugh, and at meals with the Elgars she was often in danger of choking from the hilarity and laughter that they enjoyed together, and which Alice seems to have regarded as somewhat unseemly. He had come into Dora's life unexpectedly and she soon found herself caught up in his.

It was inevitable they might meet occasionally as Alice and Dora's stepmother maintained their friendship. But it was soon plain that Elgar began to value Dora's company, and her visits to his home became

more frequent. Often they were at his request. He would write ... and she would come. She usually took the train for the forty mile journey from Wolverhampton to Malvern, but was even known to cycle the distance. She brought youth and a carefree outlook, unconcerned with the stifling formalities of the time. If Elgar suddenly decided to go for a bicycle ride she was willing, and together they enjoyed the fun of what he called 'japes'. She admired him and was in awe of his musical abilities, and she  would sit with him at the piano turning pages and listening to his new compositions, or she might dance to the tunes he played and there would be more laughter.

Elgar was an attractive man, at ease in the company of women, and expressed himself in a fulsome emotive way that could well be misconstrued. He was soon calling her Dorabella and she had the idea of calling him 'Your Excellency'. Such names for each other gave them a respectable form of address for public use and at the same time represented a personal resonance for each of them. The fact that Elgar was married and that his wife condoned, in fact at times encouraged, the relationship supposedly gave each of them a freedom to conduct their meetings without guilt or concern for gossip or innuendo. His letters to Dora and his reported conversations with her increasingly become more intimate and personal. Dora recalls long walks and rambles together with endless talk, sometimes serious but often amusing, and one special evening when, after dinner, Alice suggested that the pair went out to the woods behind the house. They sat as the sky darkened, and he described to her the sounds and habits of the creatures around. Her feelings, however turbulent and aroused, are not recorded in her memoir, but she gives a glimpse of what she felt. 'How terribly difficult to return to normal life and occupations after one of those visits. Of course I had to tell my people something of what I had heard and done but one had to be very careful.'[1]

On 21 October 1898 Elgar started to improvise on the piano. He

wondered if the personality of someone could be evoked so clearly that he would be recognised directly from the music. He thought of a boisterous acquaintance and played a vigorous version ending on a bang and asked Alice 'Who is that like?' She responded by naming the friend and saying it was how he leaves the room. Out of the original tune he had been playing came the theme Elgar used for the set of variations for orchestra which became known as the *Enigma Variations*, representing his friends in a musical form.

On 1 November 1898 he played Dora the *Variations* on the piano for the first time. All day Elgar had been in high spirits and when they returned home he 'fled upstairs to the study, two steps at a time – I after him, The Lady [Alice] following at a more sedate pace.' Dora found the first piece dedicated to his wife 'serene and lovely – and in some curious way *like* her'.[2] Then followed others in the contrasting tempos and moods of the subjects, fourteen in all. Dora got a surprise when she turned the page and saw *No. X, Dorabella*. She was overwhelmed and sat in silence, her mind in a 'whirl of pleasure, pride, and almost shame that he should have written anything so lovely about *me*'.[3] Henceforth his pet name for her as well as their friendship would be in the public arena. Audiences would be avid to know the identity of Dorabella, who she was, why she had been included, and furthermore the piece would be played in London, Germany and subsequently all over the world.

What Dora failed to recognise on that first occasion was that Elgar had incorporated into the music her slight stammer. Into the silence left at the end of the noble and grand *No. IX Nimrod* variation comes the wistful fluttering sound of violins followed by Dorabella's name called tentatively with a childlike innocence, high on the woodwind, to which one can say her pet name Dorabella, and in performance the slight elongation of the first note alerts the listener to her speech impediment. A poignant tune begins lower down, played by a solo viola, which builds up somewhat hopefully but does not come to anything. This is repeated more urgently and again seems incomplete. An agitated swirling middle section interposes and the music becomes busy and elfin-like before falling back and returning to the fluttering violins and the hesitancy of the Dorabella phrase which, by now, seems to have developed a yearning edge to it, a mild melancholy of what

might have been. There is an echo once more of the romantic theme, more muted but still present, until both fade away.

The *Variations*, first performed on 19 June 1899 in London with great success, proved a defining moment in the composer's life and put Elgar on the European musical map. Increasingly his music was performed and his time taken up with rehearsals and concerts plus demands for further works. Yet still Dora featured in his life. In November 1905 when she went down to the Elgars in Hereford for a few days, Alice met her in the hall and stated that Elgar was very busy so her visit would be dull. Dora got the impression Alice didn't want her there. But Dora stayed. Elgar was working and preoccupied. Even at dinner when he finally appeared he was dour and uncommunicative. For some reason at dessert he suddenly hit Dora's hand quite sharply, got up, left the room and went to his study. So began a most remarkable evening for Dora. She and Alice sat by the fire talking, reading and listening to the sounds from the study indicating that Elgar was composing. Neither lady went to bed. By two-thirty Elgar had joined them and played through that evening's work, when Alice suggested they all retire to bed. As Dora got up Elgar asked her to stop and talk with him. Alice's reply of 'Yes, do stay, dear Dora', seemed heavy with unsaid feelings. The ensuing conversation might have left her even more concerned and unsettled:

> 'Don't you [Dora] dare to bring any dingy, smoky frocks when you come to stay with me, because I won't stand it – and you only looked at me twice during dinner!'
> 'Twice, was it? Well, I was terrified! I simply daren't look at you for fear of putting you off your stroke or something.'
> 'At first I hoped you wouldn't and then as dinner went on, I hoped you would. Finally I went away; you'd won, and that is why I hit your hand so hard. Did it hurt? I meant it to!'
> He picked up my hand and inspected it.[4]

The next day Alice took Dora out of the house on a constant round of social calls and the following day Dora left.

By 1912 the pressures fame brought Elgar took up his time and his energies and he found a new muse in his life, Lady Stuart Wortley. Dora's relationship with Elgar which had filled her life for nearly twenty years

came to an end. When the composer died in 1934 he left behind his sole description of the Dora he knew, expressed in the only way he knew, in the music of *Variation No. X, Dorabella: Intermezzo*.

---

1 Powell, Mrs Richard (formerly Dora Penny), *Edward Elgar: Memories of a Variation*, 2nd edn. (London: Oxford University Press, 1947) p. 31
2 ibid p.12
3 ibid p.13
4 ibid p.12

Maddy Tongue was born and educated in Northern Ireland. She is currently living in Cambridge and working on the life of dancer, choreographer, teacher and holocaust survivor, Helen Lewis.

Vanessa Morton

The Sitters

Old photographs can seem overfamiliar. We see them around the house or in family albums, nod at them absent-mindedly. But they go somehow unregistered. This picture which sits on a dressing table in our spare room is like that – a photograph of two long ago elderly women: self-contained, seen but unexplored, viewed but unread.

Yet it is a remarkable photograph. I know that the woman on the left in white, propped on a pillow and looking to camera, is Caroline Murray. Her father had been an army surgeon and a respected early photographer of India; her brother was Master of Selwyn College,

Cambridge. On her right in black is Elizabeth Elwin – my great-aunt: one of eight children of a Norwich sweetmaker, and in service for over 30 years to the Murray family.

The third person in the room, stooping over her camera, is Olive Edis, Caroline's niece, the nationally renowned photographer who divided her career time and private life between the seaside town of Sheringham in Norfolk and London. The photograph may have been taken around 1930 – perhaps a little later – when Caroline was in her seventies (Elizabeth Elwin 10 years younger), at her Sheringham home.

The portrait has all the hallmarks of Edis: the main sitter placed by the window to maximise the use of natural light and its effect on Caroline Murray's muslin and lace, the two women's white hair and, above all, their faces. This gives the room itself a darkened, invalid air and the sense of sunlight and an outdoors beyond the curtain special intensity. One can almost feel that outside the house, a quick run up the street will take you to the cliffs in one direction or the fishermen's boats in another, and that the sniff of the sea would be there at the opening of a window.

Sheringham had been central to the shared experience of these three women for thirty years or more. This was a seaside resort which had rocketed from the small 'fishing station' village of Lower Sheringham in the early 1880s to a fashionable and booming resort by around 1900. The Ordnance Survey maps say it all: in 1887, Lower Sheringham had as yet no railway marked, no named streets, only nonconformist chapels, no hotel, and only the basic elements of cliff top promenades. But by the end of that year that map was already out of date with the opening of the railway and links to Norwich, London and the Midlands. By 1907, the map of Sheringham reads like a planner's dream. New straight streets have been rolled out, grid-pattern: everything is named. Gas, light and water have been brought in despite grumbles about the rates, an urban district council has been formed, an Anglican church built. The structures of seaside are in place – the Frenchified street names (Boulevard, Esplanade), two grand cliff top hotels, an extended golf course with glorious sea views and a club house. Wealthy and comfortably off families like the Murrays have bought holiday homes here, the rich and famous stay at the hotels, take apartments, the middle classes rent rooms. This all makes for a town divided: insular, long-standing, risk-ridden fishing community versus pleasure-seeking newcomers from Norwich, Cambridge, London and beyond.

Vanessa Morton

Olive Edis and her sisters would have stayed with the Murrays at the comfortable arts and craft style house, 'Claughbane', built on the Boulevard in the 1890s for their great-uncle, John Murray, Caroline's father. Edis would have been familiar with his calotype photographs, his technical experiments, and had probably heard about his London exhibitions and publications some thirty years previously. When her aunt Caroline gave Edis her first camera, she persuaded the family into letting her practise and hone her portrait-taking skills. Her early portraits – of her aunt, her mother, her sisters, of herself – were already stunning: stylish, draped, some of them self-consciously 'art'. Within a few years her adoption of autochrome colour would add to this period of Liberty-esque experiment.

But Edis, though college educated, needed a career to help support her family following her father's death. Sheringham with its different circles of aristocrats, politicians, celebrities, professional classes and bourgeoisie at play provided the perfect centre to complement the studio she had created at the Edis family home in Notting Hill. In 1902, now 25, she was in trouble with Sheringham Council for erecting a temporary studio without permission at apartments on Church Street:[i] for a while she developed the business in partnership with her sister Katherine.

The Edis business ranged from the bread and butter – the family portraits, the children, the town carnival, hotel publicity material – to the crème de la crème. By 1920, she had photographed royalty, prime ministers, bishops, generals, was contributing regularly to the *Illustrated London News*, and had been elected a fellow of the Royal Photographic Society. The dross of country house gardens and cliff scenes was continually overlaid by close-up, often straight to camera, intense portraits of the talented, idiosyncratic, charismatic – Thomas Hardy, Lloyd George, Christabel Pankhurst, Nancy Astor among them – as well as the simply wealthy, high-ranking and privileged. But these were the paying customers. Amongst the collections of photographs which remain are an overwhelming number of portraits she took of Sheringham's fishermen, lifeboatmen, and the women of the fishing community: people who must initially have been reluctant, shy and suspicious subjects, whose trust Edis needed to court, her camera and her personality enabling her to be a kind of social chameleon.

Those photographs have some of the air of genre pictures – their

The Sitters

picturesque qualities and the men's nicknames made a number of them perfect material for quaint local souvenirs. But Olive Edis's skill, mainly using the platinotype process, taking her subjects head on and often quite close up, results in an intensity of gaze which makes these portraits something quite different. They make the viewer feel as though they are staring into and being stared back at by somebody right before them. As she told an American magazine in 1920, 'the photograph ... should be the X-ray of the soul.'[ii]

This is the quality in this photograph of the two women. Caroline Murray's gaze – a little vulnerable, pensive, looking to an unknown future – penetrates the stare of the photographer (and of the viewer), quite as much as the camera exposes her. Elizabeth Elwin's concentrated gaze down at the book is in careful contrast. She is Miss Murray's helpmeet, a woman who has been in service since the age of twelve, and with the Murrays already for a lifetime – as maid, then housekeeper, then companion, now carer. Like Edis, she has maintained herself financially, has a career, a position. She is deeply accepted in this family, has been able to count on their hospitality to entertain her own nieces at Claughbane, is perfectly at ease with them and with Edis, has been photographed before. Though Caroline Murray is the prime subject of this picture, Elizabeth Elwin – Effie – seems to radiate confidence, reassurance and contentment, as though life has reached a kind of plateau.

Edis, for her part, had reached a similar plateau. She had long added film – the 'kinematograph' camera – to her repertoire, was still regularly exhibiting, taking commissions (for example reproductions for the Medici Society) and portraits of the famous, interesting and powerful. But the biggest adventures had been had. After a sequence of portrait-taking of young fresh-faced men in battle dress or groups of troops off to war, she had had an amazing commission from the Women's Work Subcommittee of the Imperial War Museum to photograph war work by the women's services in France and Belgium. On a somewhat bizarre journey, because it took place in March 1919 after the war had ended, she and the committee chairwoman and secretary had bumped and rattled with Edis's photographic equipment over battle-scarred roads.

And then there had been a commission to photograph the Rockies for the Canadian Pacific Railway – where she had had her own train carriage as her studio. She had travelled to the United States, to Hong Kong, to

Holland. But always her real talent lay in the portrait, and Sheringham remained her real centre, particularly after her late marriage in 1928 to Edwin Henry Galsworthy, cousin to the novelist, John.

One can imagine the background to this picture of the two sitters. Caroline Murray, like the rest of the family, was thoroughly used to having her picture taken by her niece. But there may have been arguments this time as to whether it was really appropriate for her to be photographed invalid fashion, even if this was just for family viewing: in past portraits she had been fashionably dressed. There would have been discussions about what both women should wear, the arranging of shawls, sofa and blanket, the choice of pose. These decisions were, it is clear from the picture, made very carefully under Edis's direction and persuasion, so as to create something of a sense of Dutch interior (one of her previous commissions). There would have been a series of shots, perhaps a few warm-up pictures (a small photo taken at this time shows my aunt with the cat), some to-ing and fro-ing, perhaps with other members of the Murray family. And then from that little turmoil this shot: two women, poised, caught, as though spun into time.

---

i **Peter Cox**, *The Village Becomes a Town: The Transformation of Sheringham, Norfolk, 1890-1910*, (Courtyard, 2001).

ii Interview, *Evening World Magazine*, November, 1920.

In addition to the above sources this piece draws on:
- the Edis photographic collections at the Cromer Museum, Imperial War Museum and National Portrait Gallery; Edis's 1919 diary, Imperial War Museum;
- Norfolk directories, official documents and material from the *Eastern Daily Press* and *Times* of the period; and
- secondary accounts of Edis and her work, particularly 'Olive Edis: From Fishermen to Kings' (Sheringham Museum, undated); S. Neale, 'Olive Edis' in *History of Photography*, Vol. 16,1992; and **Alan Childs**, **Cyril Nunn** and **Ashley Sampson**, *Face to Face: Sheringham Norfolk*, (Halsgrove, 2005).

Vanessa Morton has had a range of careers – local politics, adult education, local government, research. She has always written – but mostly for work purposes. With life writing, she is interested in the way in which individual and group experiences both illuminate and challenge our understanding of the past.

Cassandra Scott

Death and Womanhood

On the night before he died, I remember I sat on the saffron stool next to his bed, to rehearse a play for the drama eisteddfod. My father read the other actors' parts while I struggled with my lines. I stared at his beige pyjamas against the white bedspread, his fingers, the colour of dark brewed coffee, grasping the script; any distraction from the lines I could not recall. We could hear cutlery clinking against porcelain – my mother was in the kitchen.

It was late, maybe past eleven. I know his breath grew heavy, he was gasping, swallowing words, but he kept reading. He had always read to me at night, even recited Shakespeare and poetry. That night he struggled to shape the words. Perhaps it was nearer midnight when he said it was getting too late. Before he died I did not care about time. He tucked the blanket around me like he always did, and I watched him switch off the light, leave my room. He no longer kissed me goodnight, I felt too old for that.

Something made me wake. I squinted at the glaring light. My mother's face hovered over me, her eyes searching. I frowned back but then registered somebody stood next to her – a family friend who lived in the neighbourhood. She half-smiled: 'Daddy's dead.'

My father died exactly a week after my eleventh birthday. The hands on his old silver-plated watch also stopped in the early hours of Friday morning on February 25th, 1977. I woke from a dreamless sleep to a house echoing hushed tones. I think my mother held my hand down the

stairs to my brother's bedroom. Friends, neighbours and strangers were on the phone, in the kitchen, in the room where my father still lay. His long, silent, straight body rested now on my brother's bed. My aunts sobbed and moaned their grief. I noticed somebody had loosened the top two buttons on his pyjama top and his shabby slippers still covered narrow, dark feet. The previous night, and even turning eleven seemed so long ago.

The end had also come just a month after the shameful Sunday when I pulled down my white cotton knickers and spotted the dark red stain. I knew what it was. My mother had warned me for months: 'When they come,' her choppy vowels betraying her Cape Town birth, 'don't let boys even touch you.' She raised her voice to make the point that a girl had to 'look after her body.' My father was in the room at the time, he looked away. According to Joyce Moodley, my mother, a woman's most valuable assets were her honour and reputation. I think, from the moment she gave birth to a daughter, she fretted that I would lose my virginity and fall pregnant before I was married.

It was my father I usually turned to when I was in trouble. But how could I tell him? In any case he had been ill, morose since his recent heart attack. He kept to the worn armchair that had been in our family since 1945, his shadowed eyes buried in a book or in the lounge walls. His expression lifted only at news about my brother, who had been sentenced to Robben Island three months before.

I hid my secret for all of that Sunday. I was still ten years old then, and mortified by my breasts pushing out, hair sprouting in embarrassing regions of my anatomy, and now the crimson mess in my underwear. The girls would giggle at school; already they winked at one another when they stared at my chest or gossiped about my family – one brother in political exile, the other on Robben Island. I was a misfit and would always be that at school. Blood on these thick white underpants was another scary truth. I buried it in the back of my wardrobe, hoping it would disappear. Pretence was not a stranger in our family. I had observed my mother often enough confronting problems in this style. I knew she avoided arguments with my father. He was the confrontational being, living according to his whims. She was the pretender, the

peacemaker. Many years later she told me, he was too sensitive so she had to protect him. On the Sunday that marked the birth of my womanhood I also avoided my dad, as if he could read my mind. Normally on Sundays we would read the newspapers together. I would test him on the quiz questions in the magazine section and laugh at his incorrect answers. From that day on, I tried not to meet his eyes. He died 33 days later.

The next morning I crept into the kitchen. My mother's back faced me. I knew her routine; she was waiting for the kettle to boil. I hovered near her, my hands clutching the stained cotton underwear. I had to show it to her – it was a school day. 'What's this?' I asked. She began crying. I looked away at the stainless steel kettle. Our bloated reflections shivered in its belly, my eyes looked fat and screwed-up.

I remember my father's twisted lips and pensive eyes the night they celebrated the birth of my womanhood. He was a communist at heart and did not believe in organized religion but he submitted to his sisters' wish to mark my coming of age in traditional Hindu custom. My excitement grew. Since I was five, I had wanted to be like my classmates who came from religious families and talked about prayer festivals and rituals, holy ashes and Indian sweetmeats. I wanted to pray to Hindu deities and wear colourful strings around my wrists during festivals. My body's premature development though, revealed the ruder taste of tradition. My rite of passage as a new woman involved swallowing a raw egg for every morning of my period. My mother was not conversant with Hindu ritual so I escaped five days of yolk and albumen slithering down my throat. But this changed on the sixth day of my cycle with the arrival of Aunty Baikum and my father's eldest sister whom we called Periaka. The word 'Periaka' means big sister in Tamil and she was the family's sari-clad sergeant major. Her calloused palms handcuffed me, chafing my wrists. Baikum was the gentler sister tempting me with a cracked eggshell. Despite the seductiveness of ritual, my mouth was ambivalent. 'Open,' she coaxed, 'it's iron. Good for you.' Periaka, with her Durban Indian accent, growled: 'Cum an.' My mouth acquiesced. My aunt poured. My lips resisted and my hands tried to spring up to block my mouth. Periaka tightened her grip. The shell smashed on to the kitchen floor. Yolk clung to my cheeks, stuck to my dress; egg white skidded down my nose.

The truth is Periaka was the last person to bow down to tradition. She was a maverick who, when it suited her, would shift her ever-present Rothmans to the side of her mouth and pray. Maybe she wanted to believe in Hindu practice and superstition to make sense of her ordinary life, bring hope to it. Or perhaps my aunt's strong, independent streak raged a constant battle with her traditional roots and her upbringing.

As I staggered on the threshold of womanhood, she and her sister painted a white square with curves and flourishes that resembled letters of the Hindu script on the slate-tiles of our courtyard. They sat me on a low bench, in the centre of the white square and lit a brass prayer lamp. I felt like a bride. There was no priest, only my aunts conducting the ceremony. My mother smiled at me from the sidelines, but I turned to concentrate on the flames. Aunty Baikum faced me, moving the lighted lamp from top to bottom and then in a circle; she marked my forehead with a dot of holy ashes. Then the sisters sang a Tamil song to end the ceremony. Its significance meant nothing and I sat embarrassed, but I basked in their attention. There were customary gifts – a new blue dress with puff sleeves, my first brassiere and a pair of new, clean, white panties. For an instant I wondered about Daddy – inside the house, absent from proceedings.

Feasting was the culmination of tradition. On the last night of my first period we celebrated at our long dining room table. My father sat at the head with Periaka opposite him. She had cooked all afternoon. The red-brown Durban Indian curries, the long-grained rice, fried chicken and delicacies like spicy liver, curried jawbones and trotters and beans. The house was heavy with the smell of chili, cumin and clove. My aunts laughed and cried about the 'olden days' and whisky glasses chinked. They were louder than usual against my father's reserve. My mother used to say when she talked about that night: 'He was so withdrawn. It's almost as though he knew he was about to go.'

Was my father feeling guilty that we were celebrating when my brother had not even been a month on Robben Island? Or had the injustice of my brother's prison sentence broken him? Did he start to feel powerless to protect any of his children against the world? Even me. He may have been aching for the uncomplicated days of my childhood, like I was. When I was four or five he used to joke he wanted to be like

Bhima, the strongest brother in the Indian *Ramayana* tales. He would clown about, shadow-boxing: 'Who's the greatest man alive?' Knowing the answer he wanted to hear, I would tease: 'Muhammad Ali.'

We had both changed. It was the night of my coming-of-age feast and I felt out of place in my body and at the table. The adults had forgotten about me – the guest of honour. Physically, I had matured, but they still treated me like a child. I looked at my usually doting father. He was distant. I went to bed and lay awake listening to their rising voices. From time to time his soft tones pierced the laughter, crying and reminiscing in the room. But otherwise it was as if my father had already left me.

'It doesn't feel like he is dead,' I told people who asked. When he was alive, my father often came home late from his Child Welfare meetings. After his death I pretended he was at another meeting. It would finish late, long after I had gone to bed. Sometimes I would be on my way to the kitchen or the dining room and my feet would linger on the top stair in the hall, my eyes fixed on the front door. The lounge light glinted in the doorknob. I stood rigid: sure the door was about to swing open. He was there – he was about to stroll in.

The memory of a protest at Durban's Old Catholic Cathedral before he died eased the days and nights after death. We were about a hundred demonstrators, on the balcony of the Cathedral facing the Saturday shoppers and traffic on Victoria Street. I was nine and a picture appeared on the front page of a Durban tabloid newspaper of the protestors, with me behind a placard that read: 'Please Send My Daddy Home.' The grainy, black and white newsprint showed only my tiny, curly head peeping from the side of the cardboard. I was holding up those words, but my father had been there with me. The protest was to demand the release of my brothers, Strini and Lingam, as well as eleven other political activists. 'Please Send My Daddy Home,' was really the voice of my twelve-month-old nephew. I leaned against the black railing of the Old Cathedral balcony, trying to hold up the plea as high as my hands could reach, unaware that twenty-four months later I would be waiting for my dad too, and unlike my brother he would never come home. Again.

Cassandra Scott is a former political journalist from South Africa.

Annabel Howard

Nero's Different Faces:

How Influential Are Images in Biography?

In an age of spin and PR, everybody knows just how far a person's image can be shaped by the façade that they choose to show to the world. The general public are sophisticated and critical viewers of images. Yet this skill is rarely transferred away from the tabloids. Flicking through images in biographies, most readers do not think critically about the carefully constructed presentation of the people they are looking at and reading about. Worryingly, most readers also persist in the belief that they can judge character from the way that a person looks – an assumption that is extremely dangerous and generally unfounded: different cultures and epochs do not share assumptions about self-presentation.

It could be said that images are not relevant to biography and that textual argument should speak for itself. However, it is rare nowadays to see a biography published without at least a few images scattered through the main body of the text. Moreover, as readers we are often desperate to find 'a body'. Many of us skip straight to the pictures in order to visualise a subject, and a lot of us return repeatedly to them as we navigate the text. Yet it is rare to find either a reader or a biographer who approaches the chosen images with any kind of critical judgment. Biographers would not indiscriminately present letters, diaries, or newspaper articles, without some critical framework or context. I argue that they should not do so with images. They should encourage readers to reconsider, or at least be aware of, innate assumptions based on physical appearances which may often be unfounded. It seems to me

that a consideration of how these images are used is not only pertinent but perhaps also overdue.

Biographies of the Roman Emperor Nero (37-68AD) provide a clear working example of how biographers, consciously or subconsciously, use images to manipulate their readers. Nero is an appropriate subject for a number of different reasons. Firstly, he was obsessed with his image and, during his principate, images were a vital part of his methods of communication and control.[1] Nero's imagery included not only what has survived into the twenty-first century in the form of statues and coins, but also in his self-presentation as performer – actor, lyre player, charioteer, and orator.[2]

There was a reason why Nero focused so much attention upon his image: the population of Rome, and indeed of the Empire, was highly sensitive to visual material. When Nero died it is likely that he was subjected to what is known as a *damnatio memoriae* – the destruction of his memory. Not only his name but every image of the Emperor was meant to have been destroyed. The people of the Roman Empire clearly responded viscerally to visual material. The manipulation and control of images was a powerful factor in the struggle for power. Nero *had* to be self-consciously aware of how he presented himself visually.

Nearly two thousand years after his death, Nero is still a familiar figure. He has entranced generations and spawned hundreds of narratives and anecdotes. These range from the obscene to the imaginative and the curious. Whether our knowledge of him comes from arcane tales, films, paintings, ancient Roman texts, or any of the other incarnations of this much villainised and frequently re-imagined character, Nero continues to maintain a ubiquitous presence. The heady mixture that has contributed to his appeal is romanticised in the opening line of the 1924 film, *Quo Vadis*:

> Rome was capital of the world [...] to it flowed the vices and virtues of all the world. Symbol of that mixture of power and corruption, beauty and sin, was a man, an emperor – Nero.

---

1 See Hannestad, N., *Roman Art and Imperial Policy*, (1988)
2 See Champlin, E., *Nero*, (2003)

Consequently, before even opening a biography, readers have generally formed a rough judgment of what the man was like. Most also harbour some preconceptions about his physical appearance. Nero seems to fulfil the stereotype of the over-indulgent, despotic Emperor. It is easy to assume that his puffy cheeks are those of a man accustomed to gorging until he was forced to vomit into a specially designed *vomitorium*; that his deep-set, suspicious eyes are those of one of the most famous matricides in history; that his arrogantly relaxed head carriage, resting as it does on heavy jowls and a thick neck, reveals the complacency of the man who famously 'fiddled whilst Rome burned'.

This idea of Nero is partly due to the fact that biographies have tended to focus exclusively on later portraits of the Emperor: those which appear most closely to back up accusations of debauchery and megalomania. It is also because many of our judgments, particularly those concerning Nero's physical appearance, are based on a partial knowledge of the evidence, a lack of understanding of the portraits' cultural and art historical context, and ignorance of the circumstances under which they would have been viewed.

Nero lived for thirty years. During this time five official portrait 'types' were produced[3]. (See http://www.rome101.com/portraiture/Nero/). These 'types' appeared on Imperial coinage and thereby achieved very great popular exposure. Three of the types relate to Nero's actual reign, which lasted from 58 to 64AD. The first was used for the first five years of the reign (55-59AD) and is most widely represented in the evidence – six statues remain (See Image One). The second type dates to 59-64AD, and it shows a radical development from Nero's earlier, still classically beautiful features. His eyes have sunk, his hair has been coiffed, and his cheeks have swollen. These alterations are exaggerated still further in the last existing portrait bust, which was produced in the final year of Nero's reign (64AD). This is the bust most commonly reproduced in biographies, and it often appears without any reference to Nero's earlier physical incarnations. Coins seldom appear, although it was Nero's coinage that was most widely disseminated to the people of Rome.

---

3 For a catalogue of Neronian portrait busts see Hiesinger, T., "The portraits of Nero" AJA 79, 114-133 (1975).

It would not matter that only the last bust of Nero is reproduced if it was contextualised or explained. This, however, rarely occurs even in texts that refer frequently to the visual evidence. I have not come across a single biography, including those stemming from academic debates based on the visual and archaeological evidence[4], that considers the role of the portrait as a political or even calculated gesture. Despite the fact that most comment explicitly upon Nero's genuine and sustained interest in the arts, they seem to take it for granted (and leave the reader to do the same), that portraits of Nero are as veristic as unposed photographs – an attitude which seems rather naive considering that portraiture was used with explicit political intent during both the Republic and the Principate, starting with Augustus. Without exception, every one of the biographies of Nero that I have read has devoted a chapter to commenting on the literary sources. Not a single one comments on the visual evidence.

This silence is remarkable, especially when we look at the diversity of the visual evidence presented by authors. Two examples are all that space permits. In the first, John Bishop's *Nero: The Man and the Legend* (1964), the extent to which the bias of the argument is reflected in the pictures is almost comical. The emphasis of Bishop's argument is placed upon his portrayal of Nero the monster, the scheming murderer forever occupied with elaborate plots to dispense with innocent victims, whose self-indulgence led to public performances 'pathetic' in their 'ludicrousness'. When Bishop discusses Nero's childhood, rather than the beautiful child, we are presented with an extraordinary vision of the emperor[5]. He is severely bloated, his narrow mouth is turned down, his lightly painted pupils are just visible on otherwise blank and staring eyes, and the cheap marble that the bust is carved from has corroded so that his skin appears pockmarked.

An entirely different set of images is reproduced in Richard Holland's *Nero: The Man Behind the Myth* (2000). Holland trumpets his mission as a 'radical reassessment of Nero's life and character'. All his Neros are

---

4 For example **Champlin, E.**, Ibid
5 Readers wishing to see this image please look in **Bishop**, Plate II

classically beautiful, and presumably for this reason, rarely reproduced. It is the image of Nero, the 'mature ruler' which is truly astounding.[6] This is where Holland most obviously manipulates the visual evidence in support of his argument. There are not only two well-known statues which represent Nero's last official portrait types, but also numerous coins. But it seems that for Holland these images accord too closely with a modern day audience's inherent assumptions, right or wrong, about the depravity of the last years of Nero's reign. Rather than modify his argument, or seek to discover why Nero may have chosen to depict himself growing increasingly heavy and unattractive, Holland chooses the following image, indicating that it was used as a 'lasting form of public relations'. This is, again, an unusually beautiful depiction of Nero. But upon closer inspection the legend 'DIVUS CLUADIUS AUGUSTUS' can be clearly read: it is not Nero at all, but his deified, adopted father, Claudius. Holland is so desperate to prove his point about Nero that through either careless scholarship or deliberate dissimulation, he uses the portrait of a different Emperor. The portrait of Claudius accords more closely with the image of the type of man that he is trying to convey: not the self-indulgent princeling, but the wise ruler whose life has been misrepresented by those who vanquished him and subsequently wrote the history that we have apparently accepted ever since. Examples like these of Holland and Bishop abound.

I am not unaware that the argument for a more critical approach to images comes layered with problems. Every biographical subject will come with a different set of specific problems, and the practical application of these arguments to biography in general is not easy. Biographies are not art histories, and nor should they become bogged down in lengthy art historical argument. A large number of readers will not be interested in pontification upon how precisely a portrait should be interpreted. There is also a practical element to consider: how many images can be included in a biography? Reproduction costs are high and

---

6 Please see http://www.bridgemanart.com/image/Roman-1st-century-AD/Aureus-obverse-of-the-deified-Claudius-I-AD-41-AD-54-minted-under-Nero-AD-54-AD-68-gold-Inscription/499d3ad8592d411ab067cfb0113fceed?key=claudius%20naples&filter=CBPOIHV&thumb=x150&num=15&page=1

sometimes choice is dictated less by which image is appropriate, than which is obtainable, as is proved here. How much time can biographers realistically devote to images, the research for which can be squeezed into the end of a tight publishing timeframe? To what degree do publishers, particularly of trade presses, apply pressure for a strong revisionist argument which relies on a polemic use of the evidence?

Unfortunately there is no single solution to these problems: each subject demands a different approach. Nonetheless, I do think it is relevant at least to draw attention to the degree which selection and subtle authorial direction can influence a reader's mind, as this is an aspect of biography that has not, to date, been addressed.

[All images credited to William Storage, San Francisco, USA]

Image One
Type Two Portrait,
Museo Capitolino, Rome

Image One
Type Two Portrait,
Museo Capitolino, Rome

Image One
Type Two Portrait,
Museo Capitolino, Rome

Annabel Howard was born in 1984. She has both a BA and an MA in art history and has lectured throughout Italy. She is currently working on a biography of Pontormo.

UEA Creative Writing Anthology 2010

Scriptwriting

Introduction by **Val Taylor**

Whitney Austin
Chris Cox
Pamela Edwardes

James Elliott
Jonathan Gillis
Sean Gregory

It was the comedy owl that did it, this year. He hooted, hooted some more. A few beats later, he reappeared. When the scene ended, there he was. Still hooting.

A small, feathered extra stole the exercise, a gothic tale of grave-robbing. The owl, originally cast as 'atmosphere', built up his part, and suddenly, 'gothic' side-slipped into 'comic'. This is the 'snakes-and-ladders' problem of stage directions (scene directions, in screenwriting).

A perfectly-pitched detail brings the story world to life, crystallising the look of a place or object, its atmosphere, and its effect. Well-chosen verbs convey a character's energy and movement, or imply a give-away psychological gesture. Carefully-crafted phrases signal tone, style, or genre. These are the 'ladders', taking the script up a level.

In the scene exercise, there were several 'ladders'. The owl, as atmosphere, began as one, along with the dead of night, the bleak chill in the air, the old churchyard, the rattling carriage pulled by nervous horses; each detail evoking the gothic tone. But by simple over-repetition, that one detail turned into a 'snake', dropping the script out of its genre, changing its tone, unbalancing the action, as the owl became a deadpan commentator on the characters' endeavours. (Of course, 'snakes' are not always disastrous; a 'snake' in one draft can provide a 'ladder' to a whole new approach.)

The 'snakes-and-ladders' of stage/scene directions became apparent to the group when we read our scripts aloud. It's important to read out everything, not just the dialogue: promising phrases on the page can run amok when spoken aloud. This year, it was the gothic owl-turned-comedian that taught us. His cameo, though a brief guest-starring role, should have a lasting impact on the writers' technique.

The owl hoots. Again.

VT

Whitney Austin

Cat or Mouse

FADE IN:

EXT. BOSTON PUBLIC LIBRARY – DAY

CONNOR (29), of average height and dark hair, stands in front of the library entrance, peering in. MARIA (late 30s) watches him from a safe distance.

Connor looks at his wristwatch, then steps away from the entrance and continues down the street, gracefully dodging passers-by. Maria follows, jostled by the crowd. She loses sight of him for a moment, but quickly spots him buying a magazine from a street vendor. Her mobile phone rings. She answers.

> **MARIA *(on phone)***
> He's in my sight.

> **MAN *(V.O.) (on phone)***
> And the bug?

> **MARIA *(on phone)***
> About to plant it now.

> **MAN *(V.O.) (on phone)***
> Good. Stay on him. He's bound to tell us something.

The phone goes silent and Maria hangs up.

Connor stands by the vendor and flips through a women's magazine.

Maria walks past slowly, feigning interest in the stall. With his back to her she slips a small disk, the size of a dime, into the messenger bag hanging from his shoulder. She reaches the street corner and turns.

Connor is now speaking with the vendor. She pulls an iPod nano out of her jacket and places the buds in her ears. She turns it on. Connor's smooth voice crackles through.

> **CONNOR**
> How much for this one?

> **VENDOR** *(skeptical)*
> *Woman's Post* magazine?

Connor grins crookedly.

> **CONNOR**
> It's important to keep in touch with the empowered woman in all of us, don't ya think?

The vendor GRUNTS in response.

> **VENDOR**
> Three fifty.

He pays and walks off, magazine tucked in his bag. As he approaches Maria she turns her back to him and bobs her head as if listening to music. He pays her no notice and turns up the next street, WHISTLING merrily. Maria follows.

EXT. CAFÉ ENTRANCE – DAY

Connor has stopped in front of a local café, 'Dejavu'. He appraises it briefly before stepping inside. Maria lets a few people pass through the doors before entering herself.

INT. DEJAVU – DAY

The café is small but overflowing with customers on their afternoon breaks. Every table is occupied and there is a long line waiting to order. Marie joins the queue, slipping behind a larger man to give her coverage.

Connor leans on the counter and looks imploringly at the young girl, JENNY, working.

                JENNY
        Can I help you?

                CONNOR
        I certainly hope so (squints at name
        tag) Jenny. I'm looking for this girl.
        Emily? Average height, reddish-
        brown hair?

                JENNY
        Always in a business suit? Yeah I
        know her. Has a hazelnut latte to
        go every morning. Are you two …
        friends?

                CONNOR
        No, but I hope to be.

Jenny crinkles her eyebrows suspiciously. Connor chuckles, then leans in closer to her and drops his voice. The people in line behind him are becoming agitated.

> **CONNOR (CONT'D)**
> See, I met her the other day at the library. We were both in the poetry section, looking for Byron's works.
>
> **JENNY**
> Oh yeah I learned about him in school! He's the one that died of syphilis, right?
>
> **CONNOR**
> Er ... right. Anyway, I didn't have the guts to ask her out, so I thought I'd send her some flowers, maybe include one of his poems on the card.
>
> **JENNY (breathlessly)**
> Oh my God that is so sweet.

Connor grins, abashed.

> **CONNOR**
> Yeah? Only I don't know her address. And I noticed she had a cup from this café with her, so I took a chance that you might know her, and take pity on a hopeless romantic.

Jenny leans on the counter also, gazing at Connor with big doe eyes.

> **CUSTOMER 1**
> Hey come on! We got places to be!

This snaps Jenny out of her stance. She grabs a pen and jots something down. Before handing it to him she looks up, quizzical.

> **JENNY**
> Wait, she was in the poetry section?

Connor rocks back on his heels.

> **CONNOR**
> Mmmm.

> **JENNY**
> Huh. She's just more of a sciency type, ya know?

Connor's cocky grin falters slightly.

> **JENNY (CONT'D)**
> Did you see the article about her in the newspaper?

> **CONNOR**
> I don't believe I did.

She reaches under the counter and hands him a worn copy of today's paper.

> **JENNY**
> Here, page six. You might want to read it, know more about her before asking her out.

He pulls himself together. Regains his confidence.

> **CONNOR** (silkily)
> Which I can't do without her address.

He motions to the slip of paper she still holds.

> **JENNY**
> Oh! Right.

She eyes him for a second, deciding on whether she should give it to him or not.

      JENNY (CONT'D)
    OK, she lives just up the street
    actually. Big brick apartment
    building. I don't know her floor, but
    I'm sure her name's on the mailbox.

Connor takes the paper, brushing his fingers over hers.

      CONNOR
    Thank you, Jenny. You've been a
    great help.

He straightens up.

      CUSTOMER 2
    Finally!

Connor spares the man a quick glance, then tilts his head in consideration.

      CONNOR
    Actually, I think I'd like a cappuccino
    as well.

EXT. STREET – DAY

Connor is on the move again, cup of coffee in hand. Passing a trash can he drops it in, untouched.

A crowd streams up from the T station below and Maria loses sight of him. She stops in the middle of the commuters and glances around wildly.

Familiar WHISTLING streams through her ear buds and she takes a few steps forward. It becomes louder. A woman shoulders past her and

Connor can be seen up ahead, entering a portaloo on the edge of a construction site.

A few more steps and Maria has cleared the mob of people. She sits at a bench and unfurls a newspaper from her handbag, keeping the portaloo in her peripheral vision.

Through the iPod, she hears him begin to urinate. A scowl on her face, Maria starts to take the buds out of her ears, but stops when another noise cuts through. A cell phone being dialed. A gruff voice, MATTY, answers.

>*MATTY (V.O.) (on phone)*
>'Ello?

>*CONNOR (on phone)*
>Matty! You miss me? It's OK, you can say it.

>*MATTY (V.O.) (on phone)*
>Connor. Why the fuck you callin'? You ain't s'posed to check in till tomorrow.

>*CONNOR (on phone)*
>I know, I know. But things are moving pretty smoothly in Beantown. Thinkin' I can have this wrapped up sooner than anticipated.

>*MATTY (V.O.) (on phone)*
>You know what he said, he wants extra attention paid to this one. Finesse. No sloppy work like last time.

Connor sighs dramatically, zips his jeans.

> **CONNOR (on phone)**
> Matty, I am the definition of finesse.
> I was having an off-day!

> **MATTY (V.O.) (on phone)**
> You shot every damn person within
> a two mile radius!

Maria raises her eyebrows.

> **CONNOR (on phone)**
> Well, that's a slight exaggeration.

> **MATTY (V.O.) (on phone)**
> Stick to the plan, Connor.
> No cuttin' corners.

> **CONNOR (on phone) (mumbling)**
> Couldn't have been more than a few
> hundred yards, surely.

> **MATTY (V.O.) (on phone)**
> Connor!

> **CONNOR (on phone)**
> I got it! Stay within the lines. Fine.

> **MATTY (V.O.) (on phone)**
> Check in tomorrow, 2pm.

> **CONNOR (on phone)**
> Yeah. Sure.

He hangs up, takes a few deep breaths then lets out a frustrated YELL. Maria jumps as it reverberates in her ears. The portaloo shakes violently as he wrenches the doors open and stomps off.

Maria returns her gaze to the newspaper in her hand. In the far left corner a headline reads 'Local Woman Fights Climate Change – Takes On Harvard Researchers'. Shoving it back in her bag, she gives chase once more.

EXT. BOSTON PUBLIC LIBRARY – DUSK

Maria stands at a bus stop across the street from the library, where Connor once again loiters. He checks his wristwatch, then looks expectantly to the entrance.

A girl with long auburn hair bursts through the doors. She carries a large handbag stuffed with books, another open in her hands. It is EMILY.

Connor moves behind the steps, but she is too absorbed in her book to notice anything. She briskly walks off, and he silently follows.

It is a three-tiered game of cat and mouse as Emily makes her way home, trailed by Connor who is being trailed by Maria. Maria keeps a large distance from the other two, not wanting to be seen.

Emily turns down the same side street they walked earlier, head still bowed in concentration. She fishes her cell phone out of her bag and uses it to light the pages as the streetlights become more sparse.

Suddenly, a MAN steps out of an alley Emily has just passed. He is dressed poorly and sways on his feet as if drunk. A knife glints in the dim light.

The man has not noticed Connor behind him, slipping in and out of the shadows. He reaches for Emily's handbag, but before he can grasp it Connor grabs him by his shirt and hauls him effortlessly back into the darkened alleyway.

A moment passes, a sickening CRUNCH is heard. Connor re-emerges, wiping his hands on his jeans. Emily continues on, unaware.

She stops outside an old apartment building and digs out her keys, then lets herself in. Three locks CLICK into place.

Connor once again glances at his watch, and nods to himself. He crosses the street diagonally, heading to Dejavu once more. Maria pulls out her phone and hits redial.

> **MAN (V.O.) (on phone)**
> Yes?

> **MARIA (on phone)**
> I know who his next hit is.

> **MAN (V.O.) (on phone)**
> And you weren't noticed?

> **MARIA (on phone)**
> No. I've kept a safe distance all day.

> **MAN (V.O.) (on phone)**
> Nice work. You gonna report back?

> **MARIA (on phone)**
> I think I'll stick around a bit longer, see if he gives up anything else.

She hangs up and enters the café.

INT. DEJAVU – NIGHT

It is far less crowded than earlier that day, but a few people still occupy the chairs and couches. Connor sits at a small table, reading his *Woman's Post* magazine.

She strides purposefully by him and sits at the back of the room. Once again she pulls out her newspaper and flicks through, and keeps her face concealed. She hears a TAPPING sound through the ear buds and drops the corner of the paper down to glance at Connor.

He is looking back at her.

Between his thumb and forefinger he holds the bug she planted earlier. His face breaks into a cool, dangerous smile as he crushes it. A loud, HISSING static fills her ears. She yanks the buds out and he only smiles wider. He indicates the exit with his head, then stands and walks out.

EXT. STREET – NIGHT

Maria steps through the door, pulling out a gun tucked into the waistband of her jeans. She peers around cautiously but the street is deserted. She steps further out into the night.

Connor springs from the shadows, knocks the gun to the ground and throws the strap of his messenger bag around her throat. He drags her around the side of the building.

She claws against the strap he has twisted around her neck, but to no avail. He shoves her against the jagged brick wall and lowers a gun to her temple.

          CONNOR
    Anyone ever tell you it's impolite
    to eavesdrop?

He roughly pulls the strap tighter, cutting off her air supply.

        CONNOR (CONT'D)
    What do you want?

        MARIA (choking)
    Fuck you.

> CONNOR
> Oh, very original.

He digs a hand into her jacket and retrieves the iPod, then slips it into his own back pocket.

> CONNOR (CONT'D)
> One more chance. Why are you following me?

She glares at him but remains silent. He cocks the gun.

> MARIA (strained)
> What, you're going to kill me right here? Out in the open?

He peers at her, his head tilted, considering.

> CONNOR
> Yes.

The last thing Maria sees is the barrel between her eyes.

A GUNSHOT rings out.

FADE OUT

Whitney Austin was born in New York (no, not the city) and graduated from Hobart and William Smith Colleges with a BA in English in 2009. She has written both prose and poetry, but finds scriptwriting to be the most rewarding. She loves living in England, but misses her cat.

UEA Creative Writing Anthology 2010

Chris Cox

Blood Lines

EXT. CHARING CROSS ROAD – DAY

A mixed group of young ART STUDENTS come out of Central St. Martins School of Art.

JENNY, 19, carries a rolled-up banner. She's dressed in black, a stylish Goth. She has a collar with silver spikes around her neck, torn tights and artfully disarranged hair. Others, dressed in similarly distinctive ways, carry placards but it's not possible to read what's on them.

Chatting among themselves, they walk with a sense of excitement and purpose towards Trafalgar Square.

Jenny turns down an offer to help with the banner.

They walk away and are swallowed up by SHOPPERS and TOURISTS.

EXT. WHITEHALL – DAY

The road is a solid mass of DEMONSTRATORS carrying banners and placards.

The slogans reveal the nature of the demonstration. 'HANDS OFF HUNTING' 'LIBERTY AND LIVELIHOOD' 'VETS FOR HUNTING' 'BLAIR DON'T YOU DARE'

The flat caps and tweeds look out of place in London. Many marchers look like farmers and farm workers. Others have a more prosperous look about them, wearing smarter country clothes and Barbour jackets. Some are dressed in hunting clothes – red jackets, jodhpurs, boots and riding hats.

Londoners watch them pass, curious and amazed.

EXT. PARLIAMENT – DAY

Jenny stands with her group. Her banner is unfurled, leaning against railings. It is a well painted, witty image of a fox chasing a huntsman and the message: 'BAN BLOOD SPORTS'.

Marchers walk past. Between them and Jenny's group are several ranks of POLICE.

Jenny jumps up to be seen over the police.

> **JENNY**
> Animal killers!

At her words, police close in on Jenny and her group so they cannot move or see the marchers. Jenny and a FRIEND raise the banner so it can be seen over the heads of the police.

A marcher (LUTHER, 36) wearing a worn tweed jacket, baggy corduroy trousers, flat cap and old-fashioned brown leather shoes, notices the banner and smiles. The people around him, similarly dressed, are not amused.

The demonstration seems endless, stretching away as far as the eye can see.

EXT. PARLIAMENT – DAY (LATER)

Jenny and her group have lost their earlier enthusiasm. They are hemmed in, hard against railings, unable to move or see anything.

EXT. LONDON STREET – DAY

Tired, Jenny walks alone down a street. She carries her rolled-up banner. She approaches two men in conversation. One is Luther and he has his back to her. As she passes, she hears the other man, an ASIAN SHOPKEEPER, giving directions. She doesn't look up to see their faces, but walks past with her head down.

EXT. COUNCIL FLAT BALCONY – DAY

Jenny walks along a fourth floor passageway and stops outside a front door. She leans her banner against the wall, finds her keys, opens the door and goes inside.

INT. COUNCIL FLAT LIVING ROOM – DAY

Jenny's mother (LIZ, 34) is watching the news. She reacts when the door slams and then goes back to the screen.

Jenny takes off her black jacket and sits down on the sofa beside her. She looks at her mum, who is captivated by the images of country people marching past parliament.

      JENNY
  Mum …

Liz doesn't hear her.

      JENNY (CONT'D)
  Mum!

      LIZ
  What?

      JENNY
  Don't you want to know what we
  did today?

            LIZ
Of course – how was college?

Jenny watches the screen. The camera pans over the marchers and ends on her banner, just visible behind several ranks of policemen. She screams.

Liz jumps, irritated.

            JENNY
That's me! That's our banner! We're
on TV!

            LIZ
You were there?

            JENNY
I told you yesterday – sometimes
you just don't listen.

A master of foxhounds (SIR REGINALD FEATHERINGTON) comes on the screen dressed in a red jacket with brass buttons.

            LIZ *(surprised)*
Him!

    FEATHERINGTON *(on screen)*
This is nothing less than an attack
on our traditional way of life. It's
class war by Labour backbenchers –
they're paying us back for the miners'
strike. Well, we're not having it!

            JENNY
Idiot! I mean, what does he think he
looks like? Do you know him?

> **LIZ**
> So you think he's wrong?

> **JENNY**
> Of course he's wrong! What's got into you Mum? You sound like you're on the side of those ... killers.

> **LIZ**
> He may look like a prat, but what he's saying sounds about right to me.

> **JENNY**
> I cannot believe what I'm hearing.

Jenny takes out her cigarettes and starts to light one up.

> **LIZ**
> You can smoke that outside.

Jenny thinks about a row, then chooses a dramatic exit instead. She gets up, grabs her jacket and goes out of the front door, slamming it behind her.

Liz goes back to the television and the images of an invasion by the countryside.

EXT. COUNCIL FLAT BALCONY – DAY

Jenny leans over the low passageway wall, looking around. The estate is run down and shabby but has the feeling of a community. There are KIDS playing football in the central area.

Jenny takes a deep drag on her cigarette, coughs, then grimaces – perhaps she's not such an experienced smoker as she makes out.

From a corner of the estate Luther appears. Jenny is immediately curious.

Luther stops to ask directions from one of the footballers. They pay little attention, but point in Jenny's direction. He walks towards her block.

One of the kids scores a goal and raises his arms in triumph to an imaginary crowd of adoring fans.

Jenny takes another drag then changes her mind about the whole enterprise and stubs it out. She hears distant footsteps coming up the stairs and glances along the balcony. Luther reaches her floor and turns towards her, looking at the door numbers.

Jenny watches his progress with interest. His country clothing marks him out. He walks right up to her. He looks at the paper and checks the door number.

> **LUTHER**
> This is 48?

Jenny is tempted to say something sarcastic given that number 48 is plainly visible, but thinks better of it.

> **JENNY**
> Who are you looking for?

> **LUTHER**
> Lizzy – I mean Elizabeth Cross –
> does she live here?

> **JENNY**
> She might do.

> **LUTHER**
> Dark hair, '30s? – from Shropshire?

       JENNY
    Shropshire?

       LUTHER
    The country.

       JENNY
    Maybe. Who wants to know?

       LUTHER
    My name's Luther.

       JENNY
    You've been on the demo.

       LUTHER
    How can you tell?

Jenny laughs.

       JENNY
    Trust me, it's not that difficult to
    figure out. I was there too.

Finally Luther notices her badges. One, with red drips coming from the word 'blood' reads 'BAN BLOOD SPORTS', another 'SAVE THE WHALE'. He's embarrassed. Taking pity on him, Jenny holds out her hand.

       JENNY (CONT'D)
    Jenny.

       LUTHER
    How do you do?

They shake hands. It's an absurdly formal and incongruous moment. Jenny smiles. For some reason she feels well disposed towards this man, despite him being the enemy.

                    JENNY
            Come in – she's watching the news.

Jenny opens the door and calls out.

                    JENNY (CONT'D)
            Mum – there's someone here to
            see you.

INT. COUNCIL FLAT LIVING ROOM – DAY

Liz looks up and sees Luther.

There is a moment while each takes in the other.

                    LUTHER
            Hello Lizzy.

Liz is struck dumb with surprise.

Jenny looks with curiosity from one to the other.

                    LIZ (*finding her voice*)
            Hello Luther.

                    LUTHER
            You're looking good.

                    LIZ
            So are you.

                    JENNY
            He's been on the demo.

Liz and Luther look intently at each other, ignoring Jenny.

> **JENNY (CONT'D)**
> No one calls you 'Lizzy'.

> **LIZ**
> Jenny, would you please go and make some tea.

> **JENNY**
> But Mum …

> **LIZ**
> Jennifer!

> **JENNY**
> All right, no need to shout.

She reluctantly heads for the kitchen.

INT. COUNCIL FLAT KITCHEN – DAY

Jenny quickly fills the kettle, prepares the tea things on a tray and hurries back to the doorway to listen.

INT. COUNCIL FLAT LIVING ROOM – DAY

Luther and Liz are now sitting on the sofa.

> **LUTHER**
> Frances died. Sid found your letters.

Luther looks straight at Liz.

> **LUTHER (CONT'D)**
> Why Lizzy?

                    LIZ
          Frances died? When?

Luther continues to look at her.

                    LIZ (CONT'D)
          When did Frances die?

Luther doesn't want to say the next thing. He takes a deep breath.

                    LUTHER
          Three months ago – but I've got
          some other news ...

There is a shrill whistling from the kitchen. Luther and Liz turn their heads to the kitchen doorway. Jenny reluctantly goes back to the kitchen.

INT. COUNCIL FLAT KITCHEN – DAY

In a hurry, Jenny switches off the gas, pours hot water in the teapot, milk in the jug and then hunts urgently for some biscuits. She finds some and puts them on a plate. She picks the tray up and heads back to the living room.

INT. COUNCIL FLAT LIVING ROOM – DAY

Liz is crying. Jenny puts the tray down, sits beside Liz and puts her arm around her. She looks accusingly at Luther.

                    JENNY
          What's going on? What have you
          done to my mum?

Liz can't talk.

> **LUTHER**
> I just gave your mother some bad news.

> **JENNY**
> And ... ?

> **LUTHER**
> Her father died two weeks ago and her mother's had a stroke.

> **JENNY**
> That can't be right. Mum's parents died ages ago – didn't they Mum?

> **LUTHER**
> I'm sorry.

She turns to her mum.

> **JENNY**
> Mum ... ?

Liz's tears are proof. Jenny is unsettled – and then angry.

> **JENNY (CONT'D)**
> Will someone please tell me what the BLOODY HELL is going on?

Liz stops crying. She blows her nose.

> **LIZ**
> Pour the tea, Jenny.

Jenny doesn't move. She's waiting for an answer.

                    LUTHER
          I'll do it.

He gets up and carefully pours the milk, then the tea.

                 LUTHER (CONT'D)
          Sugar?

                    JENNY
          We don't take it.

He hands them their cups, then hesitates. Liz looks up at him, then turns to Jenny.

                     LIZ
          Get Luther some sugar.

Jenny gives her mum a hard stare.

                  LIZ (CONT'D)
          Please.

Luther sits down and looks at Liz. Liz looks back.

INT. COUNCIL FLAT KITCHEN – DAY

As she searches in the recesses of different cupboards, Jenny can hear talking but can't make out what is being said. She finds an old box of sugar lumps.

INT. COUNCIL FLAT LIVING ROOM – DAY

Jenny walks back to the living room and almost throws the box of sugar on the tray. She looks down at them both. Liz has pulled herself together. Luther is now the one in shock.

He takes a proper look at Jenny, like he's seeing her for the first time.

LIZ
Sit down Jenny.

Jenny sits. Liz reaches out and takes her hand and looks straight at her daughter.

LIZ (CONT'D)
I'd like you to meet your father.

Jenny sees that she's not joking.

She turns to Luther, who tries a smile that doesn't quite come off.

Jenny takes her hand back from her mother and folds her arms defensively, pain and confusion on her face.

No one says a word.

Chris Cox studied at the National Film School and after graduating in 1979 worked for over 30 years as a documentary cinematographer. Towards the end of his filming career he became interested in writing screenplays. He brings to his work a wide variety of experiences and a cameraman's eye.

Pamela Edwardes

Life and Soul

EXT. LOCKED CEMETERY, LONDON. PRESENT. EVENING

A tree overhangs the cemetery wall. The wind flips a leaf from the tree and tumbles it along the street until it is caught by the railings of a Victorian terraced house.

Loud music comes from the third-floor window.

INT. A TEENAGE BOYS' ROOM. A VICTORIAN TERRACE, LONDON. EVENING

A mirror: WILL, 18, beneath a thickly hairy wig, and GEOFF, 18, in a cyberman suit, are gearing up for a fancy dress party. Competition for the mirror is fierce. They are preening.

>   WILL
> Out of my space, man.

WILL nudges aside GEOFF. GEOFF wears a cyberman helmet, with an open face, tilted back onto the top of his head.

>   GEOFF
> Cheapskate hairy monsters don't
> mess with real-arsed cybermen.

GEOFF's helmet falls down over his face.

          WILL
          Mess with! What cyberman ever said 'mess with'?

          GEOFF
          People snap me, they go 'there's a bona fide good-looking cyberman!' Will anyone, anyone, outside of *Blue Peter* make-your-own-Halloween-outfit dudes, know who the fuck you are?

          WILL
          Off-the-shelf dude, after tonight, you'll be checking my photo in *Hello!* ... It's my birthday.

GEOFF disappears. WILL looks with some dissatisfaction at his reflection.

          WILL (CONT'D)
          It's what's inside that counts.

          GEOFF *(Reappearing)*
          Not if what's inside don't show on the outside.

EXT. NORTH LONDON STREET. COLD NIGHT

WILL and GEOFF, JACK and STELLA, dressed in their sci-fi fancy dress outfits, and AMY, with a beetle on her back, hurry along the street. WILL is struggling with a vast piece of folded cardboard.

          WILL
          Hope we don't meet any knife-wielding cunts.

> **GEOFF**
> If we do, you mediate, I'll run.

> **WILL**
> Shit, man! Some justice! A cyberman
> is thick but never a coward!

They turn into a dark and ill-lit street, pass a stonemason's shop full of gravestones to reach The Stonemason's House opposite a cemetery. A pub sign, a tombstone swings above their heads.

> **WILL (CONT'D)**
> Tonight, we are going to drink!

> **GEOFF**
> Move over Daniel Craig! Here comes
> cyberman ... only competition, little
> weed here.

> **AMY**
> Will's shirt's nice.

> **WILL**
> Present from my mum.

They enter The Stonemason's House.

INT. THE STONEMASON'S HOUSE

They greet a pair of BOUNCERS and clatter up the stairs to an upper room.

> **WILL**
> I hate to break this to you, Geoff –

> **GEOFF**
> What's that, oh hairy one?

> WILL
> Maybe, maybe, it's just the hat, but cybermen are not known for their success with women.

> GEOFF
> I'm the best of man and cyberman. Invincible!

> WILL
> Help me do this.

WILL unfolds the cardboard. He hands the Blu-Tack to AMY.

With GEOFF's help, WILL lifts up AMY to stick the cardboard into place. It forms a Tardis doorway.

> WILL (CONT'D)
> Welcome to my Tardis!

> GEOFF
> Tacky brilliant, man.

> AMY
> That so works!

> WILL
> I should have come as Doctor Who, right? Should have booked the part? Shit.

EXT. STONEMASON'S HOUSE. EVENING.

The wind blows.

INT. PARTY ROOM, STONEMASON'S HOUSE

Music. Cybermen, David Tennant look-alikes, Billie Piper look-alikes, dalek-armed boys, and blink angels dance in the centre of the room. A bar glitters at one end, an artificial fire at the other.

A DJ supervises the music. People are yelling at one another to be heard. WILL and GEOFF are at the heart of the dancing. GEOFF pushes back his helmet, he's hot. SAL leans in to GEOFF and wipes his brow with the sleeve of her blink angel outfit. GEOFF is delighted. He takes her up to the bar.

A new group arrives. SANDY rushes up to embrace WILL.

> **SANDY**
> God, my dad had to drive us right up to the door. A bunch of fucking zombies is trying to get in.

> **WILL**
> I hope you told them to fuck off?

> **SANDY**
> No way! They were the real thing!

LATER

WILL, drinking, sitting amidst empty chairs along the wall, sees GEOFF, swigging from a vodka bottle, dancing with SAL.

Jealous, WILL wades in to lead the dancers into a stomp circle. The dancers lift him up, swirl him around over their heads, and feed him up to the dais. Landed, WILL pulls his shirt over his head and tosses it into the crowd.

From his vantage point, he sees ALICE, 18, black, austere, alone, sitting on one of the chairs along the wall.

Pamela Edwardes

                    WILL
            Wow.

WILL circles ALICE. He comes by degrees to take a seat beside her. She barely appears to notice him.

                    WILL (CONT'D)
            I'm not chucking you out or
            anything, but it's my party and I'd
            really like to know who you are?

                    ALICE
            Came with the man (she nods to
            one of the dancers). Piss-head's
            gone off – don't know where the
            fuck I am.

                    WILL
            At Will's sci-fi party! What's your
            name?

                    ALICE (cool)
            Alice.

                    WILL
            Costume's fit!

                    ALICE (Eyeing his outfit)
            He di'nt say fancy dress. I wouldn't
            ha' come.

                    WILL
            Ah. Spur of the moment – (He pats
            his wig) hairy monster type thing.

ALICE looks with disapproval at the mob.

                    WILL (CONT'D)
                Bit of fun?

ALICE gives him a dismissive look. WILL takes it gracefully, and leaves her.

WILL sees GEOFF, still dancing, hot and sweaty, very drunk.

SAL looks disenchanted.

WILL rejoins JACK, STELLA and AMY. They pin him down and with felt-tip pens draw on his bare chest.

                    STELLA
                Look out!

GEOFF crashes through the dancers clutching a glass of beer.

WILL negotiates him into a chair.

                    WILL
                Whoa!

                    STELLA
                Far and away! What happened to
                Sal, Geoff?

                    GEOFF
                Honest to God, how many chances
                do you get to dance with a piss-
                happy cyberman?

LATER

WILL dances with SAL. A newly-arrived group enter and the dance breaks to absorb them.

> DARTH VADER
> Five guys out there pretending to be fucking zombies! Even the bouncers were looking like 'you've got to be mental!'

WILL spots his shirt being kicked underfoot.

> WILL
> Shit!

WILL retrieves his shirt. He sees ALICE's chair is empty. WILL looks but can't find her. He turns back into the dance. SAL is dancing with someone else. WILL heads for the bar. He dusts down his shirt, pulls it on over his head, then undoes the buttons so his body art shows. The clock above the bar shows nearly midnight. On the other side of a noisy group, the BARMAN is chatting. WILL realises he is talking to ALICE. He comes round to join them.

> WILL (CONT'D)
> Hi, again!

> BARMAN
> Hi, mate. How's it going?

> WILL
> Great thanks!

The BARMAN responds to a drink request from the noisy group.

> WILL (CONT'D)
> Nice guy.

> ALICE
> He's kind. 'N' stuck here 'til your friends is gone.

          WILL
You know, I'd be really happy if you could just enjoy my party.

ALICE looks at his open shirt, the scribbled-on chest. She walks away. WILL pulls his shirt closed and buttons it up. The BARMAN sees her go and looks a little smug.

          WILL (CONT'D) *(Despairingly)*
It's a party!

          BARMAN
What'll it be?

WILL, aggrieved, leaves the bar.

INT. GENTS' TOILET

WILL looks at himself in the mirror. Not good. Outside, a sound of breaking glass and a police siren. A blue light flashes beyond the toilet window. Behind WILL, the door bursts open as a MONSTER enters in a hurry and dives into a cubicle. WILL leaves.

INT. THE PARTY ROOM. LATER

WILL, wig on the chair beside him, is propped up against the wall. He spots ALICE sitting on her own. He looks away. He looks again. He makes a decision. He joins her.

          WILL
I'll take you out, anywhere you like. Downstairs is not bad. Or I know a pub round the corner.

          ALICE
You want to leave your own party?

                    WILL
                    If that's what it takes.

ALICE looks at him properly for the first time. She answers but her voice is drowned out by the music.

                    WILL (CONT'D)
            What?

                    ALICE
            I said 'OK'.

                    WILL
            OK!

Over WILL's shoulder the BARMAN watches from behind the bar.

WILL and ALICE make their way towards the exit. AMY shouts urgently at WILL. WILL can't hear. He gestures to ALICE to wait; he goes to investigate.

GEOFF is surrounded by the concerned. He is retching volcanically.

The BARMAN approaches.

                    WILL (CONT'D)
            Oh Jesus!

                    BARMAN
            Out! Can't have this in here, health
            and safety.

WILL looks at ALICE. AMY, JACK and STELLA look to WILL.

                    WILL
            I – I'm – bloody hell, Geoff –

> **BARMAN**
> Get him out!

> **WILL**
> He's your best fucking customer!

> **BARMAN**
> Out!

> **WILL *(To ALICE, pleading)***
> My best mate.

> **BARMAN**
> Out!

> **ALICE *(Disapproving of the BARMAN)***
> Who you eyeballing?

> **BARMAN *(retreating)***
> Just get him out.

> **WILL**
> Awesome!

WILL and ALICE manoeuvre GEOFF up and out through the Tardis entrance.

INT. TARDIS ENTRANCE

> **GEOFF**
> My helmet!

> **WILL**
> Fuck that!

>   **GEOFF**
>   Twenny fucking quid, hire deposit.
>   Twenny quid!
>
>   **WILL**
>   OK!

WILL goes back into the party.

INT. PARTY ROOM

WILL finds the helmet. FRIENDS who have heard he's going cluster round to say goodbye. He salutes them. The DJ sees him. He hits some buttons on his board.

INT. TARDIS ENTRANCE

WILL comes out onto the stairs to the echo of cheers and the *Doctor Who* theme music. ALICE is impressed.

>   **WILL**
>   Let's go!

WILL puts the helmet on GEOFF's head. Geoff retches and fights it off. Will offers it to Alice, who steps back. Reluctantly, WILL rams it onto his own head. The BOUNCERS watch as they lurch down the stairs.

>   **BOUNCER**
>   Watch out for the cops, mate.

EXT. THE STONEMASON'S HOUSE. NIGHT

WILL, ALICE and GEOFF see two police cars parked outside the cemetery. The POLICEMEN chat up a gang of young men.

>   **GEOFF**
>   Mum'll kill me!

In the shadow of parked cars, WILL, wearing the helmet, and ALICE march GEOFF along the pavement heading away from the POLICE into the darkness beyond the streetlights. ALICE is giggling, spluttering.

      WILL
   Finally, you're laughing.

      ALICE
   I's the hat.

INT. GEOFF'S HOUSE, SITTING-ROOM

GEOFF snores on the sofa with a sick bowl by his head.

ALICE and WILL are tucked up together on the sofa eating chips. They are watching David Tennant and Billie Piper in *Doctor Who*.

INT. THE STONEMASON'S HOUSE. DAWN

The Tardis entrance droops.

INT. THE PARTY ROOM. DAWN

A chaos of forgotten things; fallen decorations have been swept up into a heap.

Behind the bar, the BARMAN steadily wipes glasses. He looks up, into the mirror, his eyes blaze red.

ENDS

Pamela Edwardes worked for many years as Commissioning Editor for Methuen Drama. Subsequently, she established the Ashgate Art and Architectural History list and co-launched the journal *Visual Culture in Britain*. Since 2008, she has focused on her own writing. Her work includes a screenplay *A Free-Born Man*, and a play *Matisse: Artist*. She is currently writing a play about the work of Victorian activist, Josephine Butler.

James Elliott

The Logger and The Lyrebird
An Animated Short for Screen

EXT. DAINTREE RAINFOREST, QUEENSLAND, AUSTRALIA – DAY

A clearing deep in the rainforest, a sweltering afternoon. Atop the canopy, a SUPERB LYREBIRD sleeps, snoring. From the distance, a truck approaches. The bush seethes with insects, snakes, animals. The wind ripples slowly through the trees.

The lyrebird wakes slightly, but the truck is not too close, so he sleeps through the noise. The truck gets closer.

The lyrebird wakes, grumpy. The truck is close.

                  LYREBIRD
            (sings a birdsong)

The lyrebird looks.

                  LYREBIRD
            (sings another song)

The lyrebird looks again.

                  LYREBIRD
            (ribbits like a frog)

(wails like a car alarm)

(imitates the Windows XP start-up sound)

The lyrebird looks – no other lyrebirds for miles.

EXT. FOOT OF THE LYREBIRD'S TREE – DAY

A huge skid throws dirt everywhere. The truck pulls up by the lyrebird's tree. A LOGGER gets out and shuts the door. He carries a chainsaw and wears a lumberjack shirt and hat. The lyrebird watches the logger.

The logger revs up his chainsaw and looks around. Suddenly, in one movement the logger turns and slices through the lyrebird's tree.

EXT. THE TOP OF THE CANOPY – DAY

                    LYREBIRD
        AGH!

The lyrebird flies off the tree onto another.

EXT. THE FOREST FLOOR – DAY

As the tree crashes, the logger adjusts his hat and holds his chainsaw like a baseball bat, swinging it through another tree.

EXT. THE TOP OF THE CANOPY – DAY

The tree the lyrebird sits on starts to fall, so he flies to another.

EXT. THE FOREST FLOOR – DAY

As that tree falls, like a swordsman the logger slashes at a single tree with multiple strokes. He sculpts a small Venus de Milo in the standing wood. The tree buckles.

EXT. THE TOP OF THE CANOPY – DAY

This tree starts to fall, so the lyrebird hovers above it as it topples, unimpressed.

EXT. THE FOREST FLOOR – DAY

The logger stands in swordsman's stance, as the tree falls towards him.

                      LOGGER
              ARGH!

He leaps out of the way just in time – the tree crashes to the forest floor and rolls away.

EXT. THE TOP OF THE CANOPY – DAY

The lyrebird spies the logger dusting himself off.

                      LYREBIRD
              Grr!

EXT. THE FOREST FLOOR – DAY

The logger puts his hat on. The lyrebird flies and pecks the back of his neck. The logger, never seeing him, swats with his chainsaw like a rolled-up newspaper. The lyrebird just dodges and flies into the bush. The logger rubs his neck.

Not knowing what just happened, the logger revs up his chainsaw.

EXT. THE BUSH OF THE FOREST FLOOR – DAY

The lyrebird watches the logger, hidden, and thinks. He frets, then inhales.

                    LYREBIRD
                (roars like a lion)

EXT. THE CLEARING OF THE FOREST FLOOR – DAY

The logger bolts round to see where the roar came from, stopping the chainsaw. Confused, he shrugs and revs up.

                    LYREBIRD
                (roars louder)

The logger turns, terrified, and backs towards the truck.

EXT. THE BUSH – DAY

The lyrebird watches the logger back behind the truck and hears the door open and shut. The lyrebird relaxes. He is alarmed by the cocking of a gun. A bullet barely misses him.

EXT. THE CLEARING – DAY

The logger emerges from the truck with a shotgun, his chainsaw holstered in his belt. He goes where he shot at, now a gaping hole, and looks around – nothing there. He looks at the rest of the clearing, ready to shoot.

EXT. THE TOP OF THE CANOPY – DAY

The lyrebird looks down at the logger, who swaps the shotgun for the holstered chainsaw and revs again. The lyrebird thinks.

                    LYREBIRD
                (laughs like a hyena)

The logger cocks his shotgun and fires as the lyrebird flies away.

EXT. THE CLEARING – DAY

The logger stands rooted, pivoting to shoot wherever the noises come from. The lyrebird pops up in a corner.

> **LYREBIRD**
> (hisses like a snake)

The lyrebird disappears as the logger turns and fires. He pops up in the opposite corner.

> **LYREBIRD**
> (tuts like a kangaroo)

The lyrebird disappears; the logger fires. The lyrebird pops up in the bush near the floor.

> **LYREBIRD**
> (in an Australian boy's voice)
>
> What is it, Skip?

EXT. THE BUSH – DAY

The lyrebird smiles but realises he's stuck. The logger swings round, pointing his shotgun where the noise came from and approaches. The lyrebird flaps but can't free himself. The logger cocks the gun. The lyrebird flaps.

EXT. THE WHOLE DAINTREE RAINFOREST – DAY

A gunshot. The rainforest goes quiet.

EXT. THE BUSH – DAY

The logger looks in the hole he's blown in the bush – nothing there. He smiles.

> **LYREBIRD**
> (clicks like a camera)

The logger is confused. He turns round and fires, but he's out of bullets. He goes to the middle of the clearing.

EXT. THE BUSH – DAY

The lyrebird smiles and watches the logger.

> **LYREBIRD**
> (camera-clicks)

The logger turns to another side of the clearing, scared. He grabs his chainsaw and revs it over and over until it conks out. The lyrebird flies somewhere else, still hidden.

EXT. THE CLEARING – DAY

The logger shakes in the clearing.

> **LYREBIRD**
> (camera-clicks)

The logger clamps his hands over his ears and shuts his eyes. The lyrebird flies from one side to the other, nicking the logger's hat. The logger looks where the lyrebird came from. The lyrebird flies past, unclipping the logger's belt buckle and the logger looks where the lyrebird came from, missing him perfectly. Then the logger's trousers fall down.

> **LYREBIRD**
> (camera-clicks)

EXT. THE CANOPY – DAY

The lyrebird cups his wings around his beak.

> **LYREBIRD**
> (laughs like a human, then cocks like a gun)

The logger turns round in fear. The lyrebird flies.

EXT. THE CLEARING – DAY

The logger shakes. The lyrebird approaches behind him. The logger holds his hands together, pleading. The lyrebird pecks him on the arse.

> **LOGGER**
> OW-ARGH!!!

The logger leaps into the air, screaming as he flies into the distance, landing somewhere with a thud. The lyrebird smiles and dusts down his wings. He flies to a tree.

EXT. THE TOP OF THE CANOPY – DAY

The lyrebird lands on a tree and makes himself comfortable.

> **LYREBIRD**
> (yawns)

He stretches, puts on a frilly pink eyemask, and snores loudly, asleep.

END.

James Elliott is a playwright, and should know better. He has written for performance before and hopes to again. He is developing a script for local performance and mentors young people in the area with their writing. His ambition is to write for *Coronation Street* – failing that, for the National Theatre.

Jonathan Gillis

Secrets

FADE IN:

INT. SEMINARY DORMITORY – DAY

MOSHE, 18, a pale-looking seminary student with cropped dark hair, side-curls, a white shirt, dark trousers, and a large black skullcap on his head, sits at a desk. A paperback novel lies in front of him on the desk, closed. He looks up, edgy, anxious, thinking he may have heard something, then back at the book's cover. He looks unhappy.

EXT. PARK – DAY (FLASHBACK – PREVIOUS AFTERNOON)

MOSHE sits under a tree on the grass next to JACOB, who is lying on his back, hands behind his head, staring at the sky. Next to them are two neat piles with their folded jackets and dark felt broad-brimmed hats. MOSHE stares at JACOB when he thinks he's unobserved, admiring, and with a certain longing. JACOB catches this look. MOSHE, embarrassed, looks down.

      MOSHE
  I wish I could learn half as well
  as you.

      JACOB
  It's just a bluff.

MOSHE
Rabbi Grunsfeld told me I was lucky to be your friend. He said you were a real scholar.

JACOB
What does he know?

MOSHE
Listen to you.

JACOB
What?

MOSHE
The way you talk. Your ... confidence.

JACOB
I told you. It's a bluff. Really.

MOSHE
You're laughing at me.

JACOB
No, I'm not.

MOSHE
He said you were an *iluy**.

JACOB
Because I understand Talmud better than him.

---

* A top scholar

> **MOSHE**
> I think you are though.

JACOB is silent and stares up at the sky.

> **MOSHE (CONT.)**
> What?

> **JACOB**
> I'm just wondering what he'd say if he knew ...

FLASHBACK ENDS

INT. SEMINARY DORMITORY – DAY

MOSHE opens the cover of the book. He leafs through a few pages. From his POV we see the opening of the novel and the first words. MOSHE begins to read.

There's a knock on the door. He tries to open the drawer in the desk but it's locked. RUTH, 28, a cleaner at the seminary, enters the room. She is dark, and pretty. MOSHE has the book under his arm, trying to conceal it. She notices.

> **RUTH**
> Oh, I didn't think there'd be anyone here.

MOSHE, embarrassed, sits down and opens the Talmud.

> **MOSHE**
> I'm ...

> **RUTH**
> Aren't you supposed to be in the study hall?

       MOSHE
    I'm not well. I'm studying here.

       RUTH
    I see. Well, I'll just get on then.

She starts cleaning the room. MOSHE watches her. She sees him watching her.

       RUTH
    Where did you get it?

MOSHE looks horrified. She stops and looks at him.

       RUTH (CONT'D)
    The book I saw you with.

       MOSHE
    I was studying, Talmud.

RUTH grimaces.

       RUTH
    You need to be careful.

       MOSHE
    Careful of what?

FLASHBACK BEGINS

EXT. PARK – NIGHT (A WEEK EARLIER)

JACOB, dressed as before, is standing half hidden in a secluded spot of the park.

       JACOB
    We're taking a risk.

As we move closer, we see he is standing intimately close to RUTH.

> **RUTH**
> What's the worst will happen?

> **JACOB**
> I'll be thrown out in disgrace. My family will be shamed.

> **RUTH**
> I meant to me.

> **JACOB**
> You'll be burned – as a temptress.

> **RUTH**
> Fair enough.

> **JACOB**
> Do you think?

> **RUTH**
> Corrupting their prize student. I bet you'll pretend you don't know me then.

> **JACOB**
> No. I won't.

> **RUTH**
> I think you will.

She puts her arms around his neck and kisses him – a long kiss. Then she stops, and pulls away.

> **RUTH**
> Here. I've brought you a book.

She reaches into her bag and hands him a paperback. We recognise it as the novel MOSHE was reading before. JACOB handles the book. From his POV the book's title is revealed: *Lady Chatterley's Lover*. He looks at it, eyebrows raised.

          RUTH (CONT'D)
I read it for my course. I think it'll do you good.

          JACOB
This.

          RUTH
It's not what you think. There's sex in it. But it's serious.

          JACOB
Like the Song of Songs.

          RUTH
What?

          JACOB
Nothing.

          RUTH
Don't let anyone know.

          JACOB
I'm not stupid.

RUTH smiles. He opens the cover.

          JACOB
It's got your name in it.

                    RUTH
          Yes. It's mine.

                    JACOB
          Taking risks.

They kiss.

FLASHBACK ENDS

INT. SEMINARY DORMITORY – DAY

MOSHE, on his own again, sits reading the novel, engrossed. He stops, looks up, then looks inside the front cover. From MOSHE's POV, we see the name RUTH FLETCHER.

FLASHBACK BEGINS

EXT. PARK – PREVIOUS AFTERNOON

                    MOSHE
          If he knew what?

A pause. MOSHE waits. JACOB sees MOSHE looking urgently at him, and hesitates.

                    JACOB
          A secret.

A question in MOSHE's face. JACOB smiles.

                    JACOB (CONT.)
          Just a secret. Don't you have
          secrets?

                    MOSHE
            No.

                    JACOB
            I think you do.

MOSHE looks horrified.

                    JACOB (CONT.)
            I think I know what yours is too –
            maybe even before you do. And it's
            completely *ossur**. Forboten.

                    MOSHE
            I don't have one.

JACOB gives him a challenging look. MOSHE blushes with shame.

                    JACOB
            So, shall I tell you mine?

                    MOSHE
            If you want to.

                    JACOB
            I read books.

                    MOSHE
            That's not a terrible secret.

                    JACOB
            I didn't say it was terrible.

---

* Forbidden

> **MOSHE**
> What are you reading?

> **JACOB**
> Lady Chatterley's Lover.

> **MOSHE**
> What is that? Pornography?

> **JACOB**
> No! It's a novel, by D.H. Lawrence. Literature.

> **MOSHE**
> Literature's supposed to be even worse.

> **JACOB (laughing)**
> Than pornography?

> **MOSHE**
> They say it messes with your head.

> **JACOB**
> It does.

> **MOSHE**
> So, you shouldn't read it.

> **JACOB**
> So, I do.

> **MOSHE**
> Do your parents know?

> **JACOB**
> Do your parents know your secret?

FLASHBACK ENDS

INT. SEMINARY DORM – DAY

MOSHE, with the novel in his hand and without interrupting his reading, gets up from the desk and goes to take an apple from his jacket pocket. He sits down again, and mumbles an inaudible prayer before taking a bite out of the apple. He stops, suddenly alerted by a sound outside. He listens, edgy, then reverts to his reading, and eating.

FLASHBACK BEGINS

EXT. PARK – DAY (PREVIOUS DAY)

      MOSHE
I've heard Lawrence was an anti-Semite.

      JACOB
Well, of course. He was a *goy* wasn't he? Still worth reading.

      MOSHE
I wouldn't.

      JACOB
It would do you good.

      MOSHE
How did you get hold of it?

      JACOB
Bought it. In a second-hand bookshop.

      MOSHE
Which?

                        JACOB
                One of the shops, in town.

                        MOSHE
                Where do you keep it?

                        JACOB
                I've hidden it. You won't find it.

JACOB looks directly at MOSHE, challenging. JACOB suddenly gets up, gathers his things.

                     JACOB (CONT.)
                I've got to go.

MOSHE watches him, his face a mix of confusion and hurt.

FLASHBACK ENDS

INT. CORRIDOR OUTSIDE STUDY HALL – DAY

RUTH waits outside the doors of the hall. JACOB emerges from the hall. He sees RUTH and goes over to talk to her, his back to the doors of the hall.

RABBI GRUNSFELD, 45, head of the seminary, tall and imposing, with a long black beard, black frock-coat, and gold-rimmed spectacles, emerges from the study hall. He sees JACOB talking to RUTH, and frowns. He walks away in the direction of the dorms. JACOB notices him only as he is walking off.

                        JACOB
                It's not good to meet here.

                        RUTH
                Moshe's got my book.

> **JACOB**
> No way. I hid it. It's safe.
>
> **RUTH**
> Well he was reading something
> when I came in. And looking guilty.
>
> **JACOB**
> I was reading it last night.
>
> **RUTH**
> I'd go and check again if I were you.

JACOB runs off.

INT. SEMINARY DORM – DAY

MOSHE is engrossed in his reading now. He doesn't hear the door opening and someone coming in. RABBI GRUNSFELD is inside the room and upon him before MOSHE has a chance to hide the book.

> **RABBI GRUNSFELD**
> Moshe, you weren't in *seder**.
>
> **MOSHE**
> Rabbi Grunsfeld! I ... I've ... not
> been feeling well.**RABBI GRUNSFELD**
>
> I'm sorry. I hope you feel better.
> You're reading.
>
> **MOSHE**
> Yes. It's nothing. Just ... a book.

---

* Study session

> **RABBI GRUNSFELD**
> Can I see?

He takes it, without waiting for MOSHE's answer.

> **RABBI GRUNSFELD (CONT.)**
> D.H. Lawrence.

> **MOSHE**
> It's just a book, I found.

> **RABBI GRUNSFELD**
> Where?

> **MOSHE**
> Outside, somewhere.

RABBI GRUNSFELD looks inside the cover.

> **RABBI GRUNSFELD**
> Who's 'Ruth'?

> **MOSHE**
> I don't know. I just found it.

> **RABBI GRUNSFELD**
> Girlfriend?

> **MOSHE**
> No.

> **RABBI GRUNSFELD**
> You know this is the worst. You know that?

> **MOSHE**
> It's just a book.

> **RABBI GRUNSFELD**
> The worst. Do your parents know?

> **MOSHE**
> It's just a book.

RABBI GRUNSFELD stuffs the book into the inside pocket of his frock-coat and turns to leave, just as JACOB comes through the door.

> **JACOB**
> Moshe what the hell –

JACOB sees MOSHE and RABBI GRUNSFELD. JACOB stops, dumbfounded. They look at him. A beat.

> **RABBI GRUNSFELD**
> Come to visit your sick friend?

JACOB is silent.

> **RABBI GRUNSFELD (CONT.)**
> I found him reading.

JACOB is silent.

> **RABBI GRUNSFELD (CONT.)**
> D.H. Lawrence. It belongs to Ruth.
> Who's Ruth?

RABBI GRUNSFELD and JACOB look at each other. RABBI GRUNSFELD has understood. He gives them both a sly smile.

EXT. TRAIN PLATFORM – TWO DAYS LATER

MOSHE in jacket and hat sits on a bench on a railway station platform. He has a suitcase next to him. He looks very unhappy.

EXT. THE CORRIDOR BY THE ENTRANCE TO SEMINARY – DAY

JACOB, in jacket and hat, stands talking to other students similarly attired. RUTH emerges from the office of Rabbi Grunsfeld. She is in her coat with her handbag slung over her shoulder. She walks down the corridor, hands thrust in pockets. She sees JACOB and stops. They share a brief look. He looks away, embarrassed, and continues talking to the other students. She shrugs her shoulders and walks on, out of the seminary, into the open air.

FADE OUT

THE END

Jonathan Gillis was born in Sunderland. He now lives in Jerusalem where he divides his time between law and writing. His dramatic work (radio and film) at UEA focuses on Jewish themes, the clash of the religious and secular worlds, parents and children, and the Israel-Palestine conflict.

Sean Gregory

Reeling

                    A WALL OF SHELVES FILLED WITH TAPES DOMINATES THE ROOM. A TAPE PLAYER (MONO). A TABLE, TWO CHAIRS. A SHITHOLE OF A PLACE.

                    RATTLING OF A DOOR HANDLE, OFF STAGE, AS ALICE ATTEMPTS TO FORCE THE DOOR.

JUDE   (OFF) Careful.

ALICE   (OFF) You do it then.

                    JUDE TRIES THE HANDLE, A BIT IMPATIENT.

JUDE   (OFF) It's useless.

ALICE   (OFF) Give up, why don't you?

                    ANNOYED, JUDE GIVES THE DOOR A REAL SHOVE. THE ANCIENT LOCK BREAKS.

JUDE	(OFF) There. Happy now?
	ALICE, 25, BLACK DRESS, COMES INTO THE LIVING ROOM.
ALICE	Sometimes, Jude, it's like there's no fuse at all.
	SHE TAKES THE PLACE IN.
ALICE (CONT'D)	Bloody hell.
	AS ALICE WANDERS AROUND, JUDE, 29, BLACK TROUSER SUIT, ENTERS.
JUDE	This is ridiculous. What if he's asleep? He might have gone away for the week, Alice.
ALICE	You hear about them though, don't you? Dead for ten years, and all the neighbours do is complain about the smell.
JUDE	There's people you can phone.
ALICE	That's just it, isn't it? No one wants to take responsibility. Every man for themselves, especially the ones who look like they might need some help.
JUDE	For God's sake. (Nervous) Mister Melks?
ALICE	Shhh.
JUDE	What you shushing me for?
ALICE	Sorry.

Sean Gregory

JUDE	Mister Melks?
ALICE	He's not here.
	JUDE FLASHES ALICE A 'DON'T START' LOOK.
JUDE	Mister Melks?
	SHE GOES TO THE OTHER END OF THE ROOM.
JUDE (CONT'D)	He could be upstairs.
ALICE	Dead.
JUDE	Asleep. (Calls) Mister Melks?!
ALICE	Weird, isn't it? Melks's house.
JUDE	I don't even know his first name. Poor sod.
	ALICE PICKS UP A LETTER OFF THE TABLE.
ALICE	(READS) Samuel Melks. Didn't look like a Samuel.
	ALICE WAVES HER HAND IN THE DIRECTION OF THE STAIRS.
ALICE (CONT'D)	You should probably go and have a check.
JUDE	Me? This was your idea.

ALICE	Yesterday it was my idea. If he died in the night, that's on your head.
JUDE	We'll check.

> JUDE IN FRONT, THEY HEAD TOWARDS THE STAIRS. ALICE STOPS AT THE TAPES, RUNS HER HANDS OVER THEM AND PICKS ONE OUT.
>
> JUDE STARTS UP THE STAIRCASE.

ALICE	(CALLS) Have you seen these?

> JUDE, PISSED OFF, COMES BACK DOWN.

ALICE (CONT'D)	Look at them all. Thousands.
JUDE	What happened to going upstairs?

> ALICE PUTS THE TAPE BACK.

ALICE	Should have left you next door. Come on then.

> NOW, JUDE STUDIES THE TAPES.

ALICE (CONT'D)	Well, wagons roll.
JUDE	They're all dated.
ALICE	I know.

> JUDE PULLS A TAPE OF THE SHELF.

JUDE	Look, June 18th, 1984.

Sean Gregory

ALICE	I know.
JUDE	(READS) Kitchen? What kitchen? His kitchen?
ALICE	(Excited) Let's put one on.

JUDE PUTS THE TAPE BACK.

JUDE	And what if Melks comes down to find us listening to ... what ever this lot is?

ALICE MAKES A 'BORING' GESTURE.

JUDE (CONT'D)	Oh, that's very clever.
ALICE	(INTERRUPTING) Mister Melks? Mister, Mister Melks?
JUDE	Don't you think we should see if he's up there?
ALICE	If he is, he can wait.
JUDE	Christ, you can be callous.
ALICE	Come on, pick one.
JUDE	I don't want to pick one. Maybe it's best if we go back. Speak to someone, you know.
ALICE	And say what?
JUDE	Report a missing person.
ALICE	Just because Melks isn't here doesn't mean he's missing.

JUDE	When was the last time you saw him, ay?
ALICE	When was the last time you saw him? Should I be keeping tabs?
JUDE	When?
ALICE	You know when.
JUDE	And that was five days ago. We could have made more of an effort.
ALICE	To do what? That's why they're called loners, Jude, because they want to be alone.
JUDE	I'd hate it.
ALICE	Here?
JUDE	Not that, but yeah. I mean, living alone. The world going on without you. (BEAT) Gives me the creeps, like a mirror image of our house.
ALICE	Its evil twin. But, I mean, aren't you curious to know what's on –

SHE GRABS A TAPE.

ALICE (CONT'D)	– May 23rd 2008?
JUDE	Not particularly.
ALICE	You go back home, if you want. I'd rather stay here. Less morbid.

JUDE GIVES ALICE A HARD LOOK,
THEN SOFTENS.

ALICE (CONT'D)   Just one. Go on. One, that's all. Surely, even you must be curious.

JUDE   And then we go back. Deal?

ALICE   Promise.

JUDE   Which?

ALICE   You choose.

JUDE METICULOUSLY STUDIES THE TAPES, AS IF SEARCHING FOR SOMETHING SPECIFIC.

ALICE (CONT'D)   Take your time, Judy.

JUDE   Don't rush me.

JUDE TAKES A TAPE.

ALICE   What've you got?

JUDE   This one. November.

ALICE   Boring.

JUDE   What difference does it make?

ALICE   Don't you want to hear, I don't know, New Year's Eve 1999, bedroom?

JUDE   I'm putting this on, then we're off.

ALICE Whatever you say, boss.

> JUDE TAKES THE TAPE OUT OF ITS CASE. THERE IS ALREADY A TAPE IN THE MACHINE. JUDE TAKES IT OUT AND PUTS HER TAPE IN THE PLAYER – SHE HESITATES.
>
> ALICE WALKS OVER AND PRESSES PLAY. JUDE STOPS THE TAPE IMMEDIATELY.

JUDE Do you think we should?

ALICE Jude!

> JUDE, RELUCTANTLY, PRESSES PLAY – A HUGE BANG, THE FRONT DOOR SLAMS.

HELEN – TAPE <u>Well, fuck off then.</u>

> JUDE, QUICKLY, TURNS THE TAPE OFF.

ALICE Was that?

> JUDE'S A BIT SHAKEN.
>
> ALICE PRESSES PLAY ON THE TAPE –

HELEN – TAPE <u>Go to her then. You daft bastard.</u>

> ALICE TURNS THE TAPE OFF.

JUDE Sick. The whole room … Sick.

> ALICE LOOKS AGAIN AT THE ROWS OF TAPES.

ALICE   That's Mum. Then is —

JUDE   — us. Al, please.

ALICE   (Reading tapes) Bathroom. Kitchen. Living room. Hallway. 1986. 1991. 2002.

JUDE   Jesus, Alice.

ALICE   Why did you pick that date?

JUDE   You what?

    ALICE GRABS THE TAPE OFF JUDE.

ALICE   November 18th. The day Dad left.

JUDE   I didn't ... I don't ... (suddenly annoyed) How was I supposed to know that'd be on there, ay? This was your idea.

    JUDE GOES, LEAVES THROUGH THE BACK DOOR. ALICE SEARCHES THE BACK WALL.

    JUDE COMES BACK, FUMING.

JUDE (CONT'D)   What are you looking for?

ALICE   Microphones.

JUDE   Microphones?

    FOLLOWING A LEAD RUNNING FROM THE TAPE PLAYER ALICE FINDS A SMALL MIC, ATTACHED TO THE SIDE OF THE SHELVES

                                — POINTED TOWARDS THE WALL. SHE
                                FOLLOWS THE LEAD BACK TO THE TAPE.

JUDE (CONT'D)   This is insane.

                                ALICE PRESSES PLAY AGAIN.

HELEN – TAPE   (Crying)

                                YOUNG JUDE COMES DOWN THE STAIRS.

YOUNG JUDE – TAPE   Mum? Where's Dad gone?

HELEN – TAPE   Jude. I thought you were at that party.

YOUNG JUDE – TAPE   Dad was giving me a lift. Where is he?

JUDE (OVER TAPE)   Alice, what are you doing?

ALICE   I just want to hear her voice. She sounds dead young.

                                JUDE STOPS THE TAPE.

JUDE   How could someone do this? It's vile, is what it is. I feel violated.

ALICE   You have to ask yourself why. Why would he?

JUDE   No, I don't.

                                JUDE GOES TO LEAVE.

                                STOPPING, JUDE TURNS TO ALICE, WHO
                                HOLDS THE TAPE WHICH WAS IN THE
                                PLAYER WHEN THEY ARRIVED.

ALICE	This one was still in there, wasn't it? Five days ago.
JUDE	Will you just come on?
ALICE	How can you ... you're just going to leave? That was Mum, her voice.
JUDE	And that's why I'm going.
ALICE	I want to listen.
JUDE	Listen? Alice. Are you not finding this a little bloody strange?

JUDE SITS ON THE CHAIR CLOSEST TO HER.

JUDE (CONT'D)	I used to wonder what Melks did in here, but ... He used to sit here (points to the chair). I could barely make him out through the muck on the windows. Sat, staring.
ALICE	At you?
JUDE	At nothing, I don't know. It was weird, coming past, not seeing him here. There was always something ... I remember, after Dad left, I was coming back from the shop and I bumped into Melks. He said nothing, but his look, like he was trying to let me know how sorry he felt for me. And I remember thinking, he knows. Them sad eyes. He knows how bad it hurts. (Suddenly angry) Well, he fucking did didn't he? Probably listened over and over again. Sat in this place, his life nothing but listening in on ours.

Reeling

ALICE TRIES TO LIGHTEN THE MOOD.

ALICE: Ay, remember that time we got locked out, pissing it down, and you came round here.

JUDE: He wouldn't let us in –

ALICE: Made us sit in his front porch until Mum came home.

JUDE: (Indicates to tapes) No bloody wonder.

ALICE: I want to stay.

JUDE: Stay? No chance. (Annoyed) No chance, Alice.

ALICE: If you make me leave now, I'll wait 'til you're asleep and come back.

JUDE: I'll hardly be sleeping tonight, will I?

ALICE: Then tomorrow, when you've gone home.

JUDE: Why?

ALICE: Why? Don't you want to know what's on the others?

JUDE: I've got a pretty good idea, thanks.

ALICE: Look, and don't just get all defensive. I agree, this is pretty bloody odd. We're stood in a room filled with tapes of our lives. But ... We're stood in a room filled with tapes of our lives! What would you do if you found some old photo albums you didn't know Mum had?

JUDE   And if I try to stop you?

                         ALICE PUTS THE TAPE SHE'S HOLDING
                         INTO THE TAPE PLAYER.

ALICE   You can't.

                         SHE PRESSES PLAY.

Sean Gregory graduated from Salford University, where he wrote, among other things, a play that got made and a television pilot that did not. *Reeling* will premiere, in July 2010, at the 24:7 Theatre Festival, Manchester. Sean Gregory will never feel comfortable writing about himself in the third person.